Bill E

Follow Me!

Preaching

IN THE

Year of Matthew

DOMINICAN PUBLICATIONS

First published (2007) by
Dominican Publications
42 Parnell Square
Dublin 1

ISBN 1-905604-08-4
978-1-905604-08-1

British Library Cataloguing in Publications Data.
A catalogue record for this book is available
from the British Library.

Cover design by Bill Bolger

Printed in Ireland by
ColourBooks Ltd
Baldoyle, Dublin 13

Follow Me!

Preaching
IN THE
Year of Matthew

Contents

Advent

First Sunday of Advent
SWORDS INTO PLOUGHSHARES

Readings Isa 2:1-5; Rom 13:11-14; Mt 24:27-34

'They will hammer their swords into ploughshares, their spears into sickles.' We might think this is taking economy to extremes. Why not have a ploughshare and a sickle for times of peace, and a sword and spear in the cupboard, in case of war? Because, in the time of the prophet Isaiah, iron was a rare and precious commodity. People would not have sufficient iron to equip themselves both for war and for peace. They would have to make a decision, whether the greater danger was from war or from starvation, and commit themselves entirely to one eventuality or the other. If they needed ploughshares, they could not cling to their swords.

Our religion is about decision, choice and commitment. If we choose Christ, we cannot cling onto what St Paul calls 'the things we prefer to do under cover of the dark'. He gives a list of such things: drunken orgies, promiscuity, licentiousness, wrangling, jealousy. Note that he starts with the gross and sensational, things like 'orgies' and 'promiscuity' and works down to the more commonplace, things like 'wrangling' and 'jealousy'.

What is 'wrangling' anyway? I had to look it up. A more straightforward word for it is simply 'quarrelling.' We all know what that is; and it's not unknown among Christians. Nor is jealousy. Actually it's much easier to give up big sins like orgies and promiscuity than little ones like quarrelling and jealousy. You might think that it would be easy to give up little sins and harder to resist the big and powerful ones, but that's not how it works. The big ones are so obviously incompatible with our faith that if we're at all serious, we know that we can't have them. The little ones seem so ordinary that we fool ourselves that we can have both our swords and our ploughshares, that we can be committed to Christ and still indulge in a little quarrelling and grumbling and backbiting and jealousy. But these things do a great deal of harm in a Church, in a family, in a community; perhaps just as much harm as orgies or promiscuity.

And yet they are so very hard to give up. How can we deal with them? We can, as Isaiah suggests, beat our swords into ploughshares and our spears into pruning-hooks. 'Wrangling' means arguing; and it can be understood in a good sense. It used to mean defending your thesis in a university. The scholar who took the best degree at Cambridge used to be known as the 'Senior Wrangler'. Could we not turn our love of arguing into the willingness to defend our faith? Not to stand silent when we hear it put down, but to stand up for it, to bear witness on behalf of Christ and his Church? So many people are willing to argue about anything other than their religion; whereas actually it is the one thing worth arguing for.

Or again, that word 'jealousy.' The word Saint Paul actually uses is 'zeal'. 'Jealous' derives from the same word as 'zealous'. The two ideas are not so different as you might think. When people are jealous in love they want their lovers all to themselves, they don't want to share them with anybody. God is described in the Bible as a jealous god, who will tolerate no rivals.

Can we not hammer 'jealous' into 'zealous' by choosing Christ, and committing ourselves entirely to him? By longing for his coming, as the bride longs for the bridegroom? By keeping his commandment to love the Lord our God with all our heart and with all our soul and with all our mind and with all our strength?

Second Sunday of Advent
THE JUDGE

Readings Isa 11:1-10; Rom 15:4-9; Mt 3:1-12

Have you ever had anything to do with the law? Have you ever been up before the judge, either in the dock or in the witness box? Or at least, have you ever watched *Perry Mason*, or *Rumpole of the Bailey*, or *Kavanagh Q.C.*? If you have, then you should know that there are two different kinds of trial. The most familiar is the criminal trial, where someone is accused of a crime: let's say burglary, or assault, or murder. At the end of the trial, the accused is found either guilty or not guilty, and if found guilty, may be fined or sent to prison.

The other kind of trial is the civil trial. Here it is not a matter of an accused person being found guilty or not guilty, but rather of a plaintiff bringing an action against a defendant. The plaintiff thinks that he or she has been wronged by the defendant, perhaps by slander or libel; or perhaps someone is bringing an action against a doctor for negligence, or against a builder for shoddy workmanship. At the end of the trial the jury find either for the plaintiff, if they think the case has been proved, or for the defendant, if it hasn't.

What kind of a trial do you think the Last Judgement will be? I suspect that most people nowadays think of it as a criminal case, with themselves in the dock. At the end of the trial they will either be found guilty, in which case they will be sent to Hell, or they will be let off, in which case they will get into Heaven. But this was not how the early Christians, or the Jews before them, thought of the matter. They thought in terms of a civil case, with themselves as the plaintiff. They had been wronged, or at least they could see others around them who had been wronged, people whose property and liberty had been taken away by powerful and ruthless tyrants, and they longed for God to come as a judge who would restore their rights.

So the prophet Isaiah longs for the coming of the Messiah as the righteous judge. 'He does not judge by appearances, he gives no verdict on hearsay, but judges the wretched with integrity, and with equity gives a verdict for the poor of the land.' These people had not found justice at the hands of earthly judges, who may be apt to judge by appearances, to favour the smooth respectable person who can afford an expensive lawyer, rather than to look beneath the surface at what is really going on. The poor and the wretched will always be at a disadvantage where earthly justice is being dispensed; therefore they long for heavenly justice.

Jesus teaches us to think of heavenly justice in the same way. He tells the story of an unjust judge, who cares neither for God nor for man. A poor widow beats on his door day and night, pleading for justice. Our Lord doesn't go into the nature of her grievance: perhaps someone had stolen her property, or evicted her from her house or land. Evidently it is a matter of real importance, because she is so desperate as to keep up her clamour day and night at the door of a judge she knows to be unsympathetic.

This is the way we are taught to clamour for the coming of the Messiah as judge, to put right the wrongs and injustices of the world, to put a stop to those who commit genocide and torture and make themselves rich at the expense of the destitute.

There are some words, like 'Amen' and 'Alleluia' which are so commonly used in the Church that we don't bother to translate them; we keep them in the original Hebrew.

There was another such word in the early Church, 'Maranatha', 'Come Lord, come'. It was on everybody's lips. It's not so readily understood nowadays; it has rather gone out of fashion in the last thousand years or so. Perhaps that's because if we think of ourselves as criminals in the dock, we may not be too anxious for the judge to arrive. Let him tarry as long as he will, we shall be grateful for the delay. But if we think about his justice as the prophets taught, and as Jesus taught, and as the early Christians thought, then we will be clamouring day and night, 'Come, Lord Jesus! Come as the righteous judge to put an end to oppression and tyranny! Maranatha! Come, Lord, come!'

Third Sunday of Advent
WHAT DO YOU THINK?

Readings Isa 35:1-6.10; Jam 5:7-10; Mt 11:2-11

Our Lord has a disconcerting habit of not giving a direct answer.
When someone asks him which is the greatest commandment,
he replies, 'What do *you* think? What does it say in the Bible?'
When someone asks, 'Who is my neighbour?' he tells the story
of how a priest, a levite and a Samaritan behaved towards an
injured man, and then asks, 'Which one do *you* think behaved
like a neighbour?'

He doesn't just tell people the answer; he invites them to think
it out for themselves; a method of instruction of which all teach-
ers should be aware. Jesus knew that his questioners were very
familiar with the Bible, that is to say, with what we call the Old
Testament. They had been brought up on it, they had committed much of it to memory, they regarded it as their rule of life.
Jesus felt entitled to enquire if they had really understood it, if
they were capable of using it as it was meant to be used.

So when John the Baptist sent his disciples to ask if Jesus was
the promised Messiah, Jesus paid John the compliment of assum-
ing that he would know the scriptures and be able to interpret
them. He says, 'Go back and tell John what you hear and see;
the blind see again, and the lame walk, and so on.' John would
have known very well the passage of Isaiah where it was promised
that in the great day of the Lord's coming, 'The eyes of the blind
shall be opened, the ears of the deaf unsealed; then the lame
shall leap like a deer and the tongues of the dumb shall sing for
joy.' John would be able to put two and two together.

Jesus encourages us, if encouragement were needed, to *think*
about the Bible. To read it, asking such questions as, '*What* does

this mean? *Why* does Isaiah, or Jesus, or Paul, say this? *When* are these things supposed to happen? *Who* does Jesus claim to be? *Where* does it say that?' And especially questions of the sort, '*What* difference does this make to my life today?'

Let us ask ourselves one such question. Why does Jesus call God *Our Father*? Because, we may say, he simply *is* our Father. But what does that mean? Anyone who has tried to be a father will be all too conscious of not having made a very good job of it. Some fathers are better than others, some worse, some very bad, and some even absent themselves from their family altogether. But we all know what a father should be, and what he can be, at his best: someone who cares for his children, who loves them, who supports them, who makes allowances for them, and sacrifices for them.

Why then, in spite of what Jesus tells us, do we so often suppose that God is a bad father, or a cruel father, or an absent father? When we think about God, why do we suppose him to be a worse parent than we are? When we think about how we expect God to treat us at the Last Judgement, when we think about places like Heaven and Hell and Purgatory, do we stop to think, 'Would *I* treat my own children like that? Would I expose *them* to public humiliation and agonising pain?' And if not, then why do we suppose our heavenly Father will behave worse than ourselves?

It's a perfectly fair question to ask ourselves. Jesus poses it himself: 'Is there a man among you who would hand his son a stone when he asks for bread? Or would hand him a snake when he asked for a fish? If you, then, who are evil, know how to give your children what is good, how much more will your Father in heaven give good things to those who ask him!'

Perhaps we should meditate a little on what we mean by Fatherhood; not on the abuses of Fatherhood, but on Fatherhood as we know it should be; and see if our ideas of God live up to that ideal. If they don't, perhaps we need to revise our ideas.

Fourth Sunday of Advent
EMMANUEL

Readings Isa 7:10-14; Rom 1:1-7; Mt 1:18-25

'Emmanuel, a name which means "God is with us".' And a very good name it is too for Christ, God incarnate, God made man. What a lot of meaning is packed into those three words, 'God with us'. Especially that little word 'with'. It has, it seems to me, three meanings, and all of them apply to Christ, our Emmanuel.

The most obvious meaning of 'with' is 'in the company of'. I am going to the pictures: will you come *with* me? In a marriage, in a friendship, two people are *with* each other; they spend time together; they do the same things, go the same places. If a marriage or a friendship is broken by death, or a divorce, or a quarrel, people miss more than anything the simple *presence* of the other person. We would give anything to have that person back, simply to be there *with* us. We read in the Book of Genesis that God was *with* Adam and Eve in the Garden of Eden. He walked with them in the cool of the evening, he shared their paradise, shared their world. That intimacy was broken by sin; mankind endured as it were a bereavement, or a divorce from God; but we find the intimacy restored in Christ. Once more God walks on our hills, beside our rivers; he shares our experience, keeps us company. He eats and drinks with us, talks with us, as a man talks to his friend. God is with us.

But that little word 'with' has another meaning. A lecturer may pause in the middle of a complicated explanation and say, 'Are you with me?' That is to say, 'Do you understand me?' Now we are very complicated beings. We scarcely understand ourselves. How can anybody else begin to understand the complexity of our motives, our thoughts, our actions? I try to prepare a good Confession. Did I really mean that hurtful remark, or did it just slip out in the heat of the moment? I scarcely know, I scarcely have that degree of insight into my own character.

Does God really understand us, through and through? Yes, of course he does. As our Creator, he knows by name every atom that has gone into us, he knows our thoughts and motives infinitely better than we do ourselves. But more than this, he has got to know us, intimately, from the inside, by becoming one of us. He has learned to feel compassion for human suffering, he has felt that wrenching ache in his stomach as he looked at the man deformed by leprosy, or listened to the hysterical sobbing of the woman whose only son had died. He has felt the warm glow imparted by human goodness, as he saw the widow give her last coins to the Temple, to serve God's glory. And he has felt, too, the very real limitations of human goodness, the extent to which evil has corrupted and deformed our natures. He felt that very clearly in the nails which pierced his hands, in the scourge which bit into his back, in the thorns which raked his head, in the spittle which defiled his face. Yes, God in Christ knows all there is to know about us; in that sense too, he is God with us.

And there is a third sense to that little word 'with'. My father fought with Monty: not against him, but on his side. If God is with us, who can be against us? There is a story in the Second Book of Kings. The King of Syria sent an army to arrest the prophet Elisha. When Elisha's servant looked out, he saw that they were surrounded by an army with horses and chariots. He said to Elisah, 'What shall we do?' Elisha said, 'Do not be afraid, for those that are with us are more than those that are with them.' And his servants eyes were opened, and he saw that the mountain was full or horses and chariots of fire - the army of the Lord. Too often in our lives, things go badly wrong. We lose our partners, our friends, our jobs, our self-esteem. Things are against us. Nevertheless, those that are with us are more than those who are against us, for God is with us, he will send us his angels to watch over us. He has sent us more than his angels, he has sent us his Son, Emmanuel, God-with-us. Christ is with us, at our side, on our side, showing God's solidarity with us, whether we face injustice, or spite, or misunderstanding, or calamity, even when we try to face up to the less pleasant aspects of our own character. He fights with us; not against us, but on our side, against oppression, against our weakness. Come, Emmanuel, God's presence among us, our King, our Judge, save us, Lord our God!

The Season of Christmas

Christmas
LIGHT

Readings
Midnight Mass: Isa 9:1-7; Tit 2:11-14; Lk 2:10-11
Dawn Mass: Isa 62:11-12; Tit 3:4-7; Lk 2:15-20
Day Mass: Isa 52:7-10; Heb 1:1-6; Jn 1:1-18

From the Prophet Isaiah: 'The people that walked in darkness has seen a great light; on those who live in a land of deep shadow, a light has shone.' Or again from St John's Gospel: 'A light shines in the dark, a light that darkness could not overpower.' Again and again in the scriptures the birth of our Saviour is described as a light shining in the darkness. The shepherds are out in the fields, keeping watch over their flocks at night; a dangerous time for shepherds, for night is the time when a wolf may sneak up unseen and steal one of the sheep; or the sheep, or indeed the shepherd himself, may fall over a cliff, invisible in the darkness. And suddenly, into this darkness of anxiety and danger, a great light shines: the glory of the Lord shines all around them, and the angel of the Lord appears to announce the birth of Christ, the Christ who is the Rising Sun who will give light to those who live in darkness and the shadow of death.

All over the world at this time there is great darkness: the darkness of the shadow of death for many people whose countries are at war, or who are torn apart by internal strife; those who are diseased or starving in countries where there are no medical facilities and little food; the darkness of despair for those who are homeless and for those who are imprisoned for what they believe. For people such as this, we ourselves are called to be the light in their darkness, we ourselves are called to be their Christmas. When Christ told his disciples that they were the light of the world, he was not paying them a compliment, telling them that they were decent fellows. He was giving them a commandment: get out there and bring my light to those in darkness. We are the light of the world, you and I. How much light are we bringing to the world this Christmas? How many people are blessing us because we have brought light into their darkness?

But we also have darkness in our own lives. You and I both live in darkness still, a darkness that needs to be illuminated ever more and more by the light of Christ. Each of us has our share of darkness, and for each of us the darkness is different. Some may have the darkness of grief, having lost a loved one, trying to face life alone. Others may face the darkness of illness, the fear that the cancer is not going to get better or go away. Others may have deep and dark worries over the future, having lost a job or been threatened with its loss. Some may be staring into the darkness of guilt, a deep consciousness of things that should have been done better, or should not have been done at all. Some live in the darkness caused by loss or weakening of their Faith.

To all of us, and in every kind of darkness, the light of Christ shines anew. The message of Advent has been, 'Awake, O sleeper, and rise from the dead, and Christ will give you light.' Christ gave sight to the blind, he healed the lepers, forgave the thief on the cross, brought the dead back to life. There is nothing in our situation which he cannot deal with, no corner of our darkness into which he cannot shed his glorious light. This is the promised Sun of Righteousness, who is rising with healing in his wings. This is the light of the world, the light which is the life and hope and joy of men and women all over the world, the radiant light of God's glory, the glory of the only Son of the Father, full of grace and truth.

Sunday in the Octave of Christmas
THE HOLY FAMILY

Readings Eccus 3:2-6.12-14; Col 3:12-21; Mt 2:13-15.19-23

Once, when I was in charge of a rather rough inner-city parish, I was asked to fill in a questionnaire about church attendance. One question was, 'How many families do you have in your congregation?' I was sorely tempted to write, 'Not applicable.' Because actually I didn't have any families at all in my congregation. I had spinsters, I had widows; I had married women, but they didn't bring their husbands. I had married men, but they didn't bring their wives. I had parents, but they didn't bring their children. I had children, but they didn't bring their parents. I had every sort of person, but what I didn't have was one complete family, with two parents and two point four children.

There were in fact few such families in my parish. There were single mothers bringing up children; there were families consisting of stepfathers, half-sisters, grandmothers acting as foster-mothers, and every sort of irregular, temporary, makeshift relationship; but of what we like to regard as the normal family, there were very few.

For a lot of people today the idea of a feast of the ideal family may be slightly irritating. The icon of the man, the woman and the baby, bonded together by love, is very alien to a lot of people's experience. A celebration of the sanctity of family life must be a strange and off-putting thing to people all too aware of the imperfections of their own family life.

But was the life of the Holy Family so ideal? Certainly it was very far from normal. Remember that Joseph is not Jesus's father. How many virgins have babies? How many men are asked to act as foster-father to the Son of God? Joseph has taken responsibility for a child not his own. And now he is told to take the child and its mother to Egypt, because the king is trying to kill the child. A lot of men would have responded by procuring a very quick divorce. They would have said, 'The king wants to kill your child. That's *your* problem; he's not *my* child.' A less responsible man than Joseph would have abandoned Mary and Jesus there and then, and gone off to Egypt himself, out of harm's way.

We make a lot of Mary in the Catholic Church. It can be sobering to turn to the Bible and find how little is said about her character. We like to think of her as loving, affectionate, serene; but that is merely surmise. Still less is said about the character of Joseph. We don't know if he was an indulgent step-father, or a harsh and severe one; the Bible just doesn't say. What *is* very clear from the actions of Joseph and Mary is that they took their responsibilities seriously. They stand as a model, not so much for ideal, 'normal' families, but for irregular families, single-parent families, families where the grandparents are the virtual parents, all kinds of families which have only this in common: that the members of the group, however incomplete, unsatisfactory and makeshift it may be, take responsibility for one another and try to do their very best for one another in very difficult circumstances, and at great personal cost.

Saint Paul's advice to the families of Colossae becomes more acceptable if we realise that Paul was writing to real people, people he knew, of whose limitations he was perfectly aware. 'Wives, give way to your husbands.' That has been taken by some men as saying that men are the superior sex, and resented by women for that reason. That's not what Paul meant. He knew those husbands and wives; he knew how brutal and coarse those men could be; he knew how resentful and obstinate their wives could be. But coarse brutality coupled with obstinate resentment do not make for happy families. Someone has to give way. He goes on, 'Husbands, love your wives and treat them with gentleness.' A novel idea, I imagine, for some of those husbands. 'Children, be obedient to your parents … Parents, never drive your children to resentment.' What obvious and elementary advice! You don't need to give such advice to ideal families. But Colossae was not populated with ideal families; neither are our modern parishes. The life of the Holy Family, and the writings of St Paul, do not present an impossibly high standard to discourage those incapable of matching it; they offer a way forward to very real families with very real problems and difficulties; families like ours.

Second Sunday after Christmas
GOD'S WORD

Readings Eccus 24:1-2.8-12; Eph 1:3-6.15-18; Jn 1:1-18

Do you have a favourite word? Or, is there a word that you really dislike? Are there words which are banned from your house? Words are very powerful things, for good or evil. The old proverb says, 'Sticks and stones will break my bones, but names will never hurt me;' but that's not true. Names, like any other words, have great power to hurt. They also have great power to do good. We all know the three little words, 'I love you.' There are also magic words. When I was a child I was taught that if you wanted a sweet, you had to use the magic words, 'Please' and 'Thank you.'

What would God's word sound like? That's a silly question; we all know what God's word sounds like. At every Mass we read a passage or two from the Bible, and we say, 'This is the Word of the Lord.' But why is the Book of Isaiah, or the letter of St Paul to the Ephesians, called 'The Word of the Lord?' What makes it different from any other word? Why is it *God's* word?

Because it expresses God's meaning. It shows us who God is, and what God is. We can't see God, but we can hear his word. Moses wanted to see God, but God wouldn't allow that. Instead he pronounced his name in Moses' hearing, 'The Lord, the Lord, a God merciful and gracious, slow to anger, and abounding in steadfast love and faithfulness.' These are words which reveal God, show us what he is like, reveal his will and purpose and character.

Saint John tells us that in Jesus, the Word of God became flesh, and dwelt among us. In Jesus then we *can* see God. We see revealed in him the wisdom and the power and the love and the forgiveness and the patience and the greatness and the humility of God. How do we see these things revealed? In the manger we see the humility of God; the God who created the earth and the heavens and all they contain is content to be born a baby in the most humble surroundings. In the earthly ministry of Jesus, we see the wisdom of God as Jesus speaks the most sublime and glorious words to his followers. We see the love and power of God as he restores sight to the blind and hearing to the deaf, and life itself to those who have died. On the cross we see the patience and the forgiveness of God: 'Father, forgive them, for they know not what they do.' In the resurrection and the ascension we see the power and the greatness of God. In the birth and life and death and resurrection of Jesus, in our whole experience of Christ, we see the Glory of God, the Glory of the only Son of the Father, full of grace and truth.

The Epiphany of the Lord
EPIPHANY

Readings Isa 60:1-6; Eph 3:2-3.5-6; Mt 2:1-12

One of the most necessary social skills is being able to say nice things about someone else's baby. Isn't he big for his age! What beautiful hair she has! And mothers appreciate it. I've never yet met a mother who didn't like showing off her baby. I'm sure Mary enjoyed showing off Jesus to the Wise Men who had come so far to see him. The word Epiphany means 'showing off'. There's a posher translation, 'Manifestation' but that's a rather learned word to describe what a mother does with her baby. 'Where have you been this morning, my dear?' 'I've been round the mums' and toddlers' group, manifesting my baby' - She's been doing nothing of the kind, she's been showing her baby off.

The first and foremost task of the Church is to show Jesus off.

We can't expect people nowadays to follow a star halfway round the world and find a baby in a stable. If they are going to see Jesus at all it must be because you and I have shown them Jesus. I was shown Jesus by other Christians; I can think of several people who might claim the title to be my personal Epiphany, people who showed me Jesus. That is what Christians are for. When Andrew told his brother Peter, 'We have found the Christ', and took him to Jesus, he was an Epiphany to Peter.

It is my very special privilege as a priest to be an Epiphany at every Mass. I hold up the Host and say, 'This is the Lamb of God who takes away the sins of the world.' I lift up your Saviour and show him to you. In the same way, when the Wise Men came to Bethlehem asking, 'Where is he who is born king of the Jews?' we can imagine Mary lifting up Jesus and showing them, and saying, 'This is the one you have come to see.' Mary was the first Epiphany and she remains the Epiphany, showing her Son to the world, saying as she said at Cana in Galilee and as she has said at so many appearances since, 'This is my Son. Listen to Him. Do whatever He says.'

Are *we* an Epiphany? Do we show Jesus to our families, our friends, our workmates? Are there people in the world who could say to us, 'I know Jesus because *you* showed him to me, *you* were my Epiphany?' How would we do that? There are special ways in which Jesus wants us to be his Epiphany. We can show people our Faith. 'I believe in one Lord Jesus Christ. I believe that the Son of God has become a Man and died on a cross to redeem me by his blood. That belief influences my whole life. I believe that all people are very precious, because God has made them and Christ has died for them.'

We can show people our Hope. 'I look for the resurrection of the Dead and the Life of the world to come. I hope to spend eternity gazing in joy beyond expression at the face of God. That hope gives me a different perspective on this life, it changes the way I look at everything.'

We can show people our Love, the love which Jesus showed, the total, self-denying love of Calvary. How wonderful if someone were able to say to us, 'How is it that you love so much, that you love even people who do not love you?' And we were able to reply, 'Any love we have is the gift of Christ the Lord. We love because he first loved us. If you see his love in us, then you are seeing Christ.' If we are ever able to say that, we shall *be* the Epiphany.

The Baptism of the Lord
THE CRUSHED REED

Readings Isa 42:1-4.6-7; Acts 10:34-38; Mt 3:13-17

'He does not break the crushed reed, nor quench the wavering flame.' I wonder what those words mean to you? They suggest to me someone infinitely gentle, infinitely careful not to harm the damaged and the vulnerable. Human beings can rarely be that gentle. We go to war for the best of causes, to defend the lives and rights of the innocent, but inevitably some of those innocent people get hurt in the process. We have a saying, 'You can't make an omelette without breaking eggs' - which means that too often in our zeal to reform, the crushed reed is broken off, the wavering flame is snuffed out. The only people who never harm anybody are those who never undertake anything worthwhile.

Except, that is, for Jesus, who undertakes nothing less than the salvation of the world, but who does so with infinite care for the weak, the foolish, the misguided. If ever a man brought trouble on himself, it was the man who arrested Jesus, and got his ear cut off in the process; yet Jesus touches the ear, and heals it. If ever a man deserved contempt and rejection, it was Peter, when he denied Jesus three times; yet Jesus forgives him and makes him shepherd of his flock. If ever men deserved punishment, it was those who crucified Jesus; yet Jesus says, 'Father, forgive them.'

'He does not quench the wavering flame.' Peter was a wavering flame, faltering when he should have borne witness to Jesus. But which of us is not a wavering flame? Which of us burns as brightly as we should? Which of us does not fail, from time to time, to bear witness to Jesus? Would not Jesus be justified in blowing us out, and lighting some other flame? But for Jesus, nobody is so morally weak that he can be snuffed out; he is always trying to fan that feeble little spark of goodness into flame.

How grateful we should be for the gentleness, the patience, the forbearance, of Jesus! May he continue to bear with us, and encourage and strengthen the goodness within us, until, as the prophet says, true justice is established on earth, and he has completed his mission to open the eyes of the blind, to free the captives from prison, and those who live in darkness from the dungeon; until he has established his kingdom of freedom, love, and truth.

Lent

First Sunday of Lent
TEMPTATION

Readings Gen 2:7-9; 3:1-7; Rom 5:12-19; Mt 4:1-11

'The woman saw that the tree was good to eat, and pleasing to the eye, and that it was desirable for the knowledge that it could give.' The devil never fights fairly. He sends, not one temptation, but a whole cluster of them, so that even if you resist one, you fall to another. The fruit tempted the woman through her appetite and sense of taste, for it was good to eat. It tempted her through the sense of sight, for it was pleasing to the eye. It aroused her curiosity, for it was desirable for the knowledge that it could give. Doubtless also it excited her, because forbidden fruit is always sweeter. Doing something forbidden in itself confers a certain pleasure, whatever other benefits it may or may not bring us; a fact well known to every vandal.

Consider the sad story of Sharon – and I'd better say before I start that Sharon is entirely fictious. I intend no similarity to any living person. Sharon was well brought up, with excellent Catholic principles. She was in no way inclined to drunkenness, or to promiscuity. But she contracted an unhappy marriage. Her husband was a brute, who beat her, did not let her go out, and was unfaithful to her. It happened one day that her husband was away on a business trip. Her friend Alice invited her out to a night club. Sharon hadn't been out at all, let alone to a night-club, for years. So she went. She had a couple of drinks, and then a couple more. A young man asked her to dance, and then asked her back to his place; and they ended up in bed.

Afterwards Sharon was overcome with guilt and went to confession. She confessed to drunkenness and having extra-marital sex. Now both of those are serious sins, and the Church does not condone them, but I dare say that all of us can see things from

Sharon's point of view. She had been bombarded with temptations from every side: the anger and shame and frustration at her husband's behaviour, the desire for revenge, the feeling of liberation on getting a night out, the loosening effect of a couple of drinks, the young man's charm and good looks. She could have resisted any one of those temptations by itself, but they all came at once, and they were too much for her. How would *we* have behaved if subjected to all these temptations? Nobody who has ever felt temptation will be inclined to cast the first stone.

I think we should take very seriously the story of Jesus being tempted in the wilderness. The Son of God allows himself to experience temptation: the weakening effects of hunger; the desire to show himself for who he is, the Son of God; the desire for worldly power and prestige and authority. I wonder if those experiences came as a shock to Jesus. They are described as temptations, and that means that for a time at least he really wanted to do those things: he really fancied throwing himself off the temple and having the angels carry him safely to the ground. That would show the people of Jerusalem a thing or two! He thought how wonderful it would be to be king of all the world; had he not made it all himself?

He did not, of course, give in to those temptations; but he now understood very well the *power* of temptation. He included a petition against temptation in his prayer: 'Lead us not into temptation.' He knew well that others would not be able to resist it as well as himself. He was understanding to the point of indulgence towards those who had *not* been able to resist temptation. He does not throw a stone at the woman taken in adultery, he tells her '*I* do not condemn you; go away and sin no more.' He does not reproach his disciples after they run away from Gethsemane. He does not condemn Peter for denying him three times. He even makes excuses for those who crucified him: 'Father, forgive them,' he says, 'for they know not what they do.'

I wonder why so few people nowadays make use of the sacrament of reconciliation. Have people stopped giving in to temptation? I hardly think so. Or do we suppose that we shall find there a God who does not make allowance for our failings? Surely not; God knows our weakness very well. He is not determined to make much of our sins and punish us for them; if he were, he would not have sent his Son to die for their forgiveness.

Second Sunday of Lent
EXPERIENCING GOD

Readings Gen 12:1-4; 2 Tim 1:8-10; Mt 17:1-9

Recently I attended an ecumenical study group. We listened to a tape about the experience of God. There were a number of speakers on the tape, including two very eminent churchmen. Both of them said that they had never had a direct experience of God. By that, I suppose they meant that they had never experienced anything like the disciples experienced on the Mount of the Transfiguration: Jesus, shining in glory, acknowledged by the voice of God from heaven, witnessed to by Moses and Elijah.

I'm not sure how helpful it was to talk about experience of God in those terms. Not many people do have such experiences; and I felt that our discussion group, invited to think of experience of God in that way, decided that they themselves had never had any experience of God. But of course they had. They were underestimating the value of their own experiences. Experience of God is very common, though it takes many forms. Many of us will have been moved by a passage from the scriptures, or even by a sermon, and thought, 'That word was for me; that was a message to me from God.' And so it was. Or again, many of us, perhaps in prayer, perhaps during a walk in the country, perhaps sitting quietly at home, have experienced a presence, which we have interpreted as the presence of God; and we were right to interpret it so. We may have experienced God's comfort in bereavement, or his strength helping us in our weakness. We may have come through a difficult situation and realised that we could not have done this by ourselves; and all these are perfectly real, and very valuable, experiences of God.

Let's go back to the disciples on the mountain. They see Jesus transfigured, they see Moses and Elijah, they hear the voice of God saying, 'This is my Son, Listen to him.' No doubt from that moment on they did listen to Jesus with particular attention. But he had *always* been the Son of God; the words he had spoken to them had *always* been the words of God, even before this was pointed out to them on the mountain. When he had said to them, 'Blessed are the poor in spirit,' or when he had said, 'Love your enemies, and pray for those who persecute you,' or when he had taught them to pray, 'Our Father who art in heaven,' they had been having a very real and very direct experience of God. They had been hearing the words of God; indeed, they had been encouraged to *speak* the very words of God. For what are we doing when we pray the Lord's Prayer if we are not speaking to God in his own words, speaking to him, as it were, in his own language?

Now *we* can have this experience of God just as surely as the disciples did. We can hear the word of God any time we choose to come to church, any time we care to open a bible. But, just like the disciples, we can underestimate the value of our experience. The disciples had been listening to Jesus for a long time before the value and the importance of listening to him was pointed out to them on the mountain. They had argued about what he said, or disagreed with him, or showed by their conduct that his words had had little effect on them. When the disciples were arguing on the road about which of them was the greatest, had they been listening to a word he said about humility? When they suggested that he call down fire from heaven upon the Samaritan village, had they been listening to what he said about forgiveness?

We too, can hear the words of God as though they were a bit of idle gossip, and do nothing about them. That was not what Abram did. The Lord said to Abram, 'Leave your country, your family and your father's house.' And the story goes on, 'So Abram went as the Lord told him.' He obeyed. Are we so ready to obey? When God tells us, 'Love your neighbour' or 'Forgive your enemies' or 'Take no thought for the morrow' – do we listen? Do we obey? Or do we suppose that these words were directed at people who lived long ago, in a world very different from our own?

Third Sunday of Lent
THE WOMAN AT THE WELL

Readings Ex 17:3-9; Rom 5:1-2.5-8; Jn 4:5-42

The Holy Land contains two very different regions, Judea and Galilee. Judea is mountainous and dry and dusty, Galilee is lush and green, with plenty of water. The two regions are about fifty miles apart, and between them lies Samaria. Nowadays Samaria be a dangerous place to pass through, because of the animosity between Jews and Palestinians. Some tour operators think it wiser to avoid Samaria altogether, by taking the long way round, through the Jordan valley. I wouldn't recommend that road to anyone; it's twice as long as the direct route, a weary, winding, monotonous mountain road.

The long way round wasn't available to Jesus. Without metalled roads and motor coaches, the only possible route was through Samaria. As St John remarks, he *had* to cross Samaria. He might have preferred not to do so, because then as now, the inhabitants of Samaria were hostile to the Jews.

Jesus was, we are told, leaving Judea because of the jealousy of the Pharisees. No doubt he set out on the journey with some disappointment in his heart, some sense of rejection and failure. Things had been going well, but then the blindness and envy of the religious leaders of his own people had made things difficult for him. The road through Samaria was long, the country was semi-desert: very hot, very dry. And he was passing through hostile territory. At last they reached Jacob's well, near the town of Sychar. The disciples went on into the town to buy bread, but Jesus was too tired, and perhaps too dejected, to go any further. So he sat down beside the well.

A woman came along to draw water from the well, and Jesus asked her for a drink. Scholars have pointed out how remarkable it was that Jesus should have spoken to a woman, and a Samaritan woman at that, breaking down barriers between sex, race and religion. Maybe so; but let's not overlook the obvious point that Jesus had no option. He was at the end of his tether; he was worn out, the day was hot, he was thirsty. He needed a drink. He had no bucket of his own, and perhaps not much strength left. His disciples had gone into town. There was no one around but the woman, and if he wanted a drink, he had to ask her for one.

His request led to a conversation with that woman, quite a remarkable conversation. As a result of it, she was converted to the gospel, and not only her, but all the people of her village. It had a very considerable effect on their lives. And yet it came about because Jesus was tired, and thirsty, and dejected. In other words he was doing his Father's will simply by accepting the limitations and frustrations of the human condition, being subject to tiredness and thirst and the human feelings of rejection and failure. And that I take it is a great part of the meaning of the Incarnation. The Son of God comes to live among us in the limitations of weakness, and it is that very weakness which furthers his Father's purposes.

I would hope that this reflection might give us courage when we come up against our own weakness: when we feel too tired to go on, or feel that we have failed, perhaps when we been made redundant or had some dreadful disappointment; when we are sick, find that we have some incurable illness; when our marriage breaks up, or our children seem to reject us and we feel that all our life's work has been in vain. It is at these very moments, if we can but see it, that God can use us and bring about his kingdom through us.

Fourth Sunday of Lent
THE LIGHT OF THE WORLD2

*Readings*1 Sam 16:1.6-7.10-13; Eph 5:8-14; Jn 9:1-41

I wonder if you've ever taken the trouble to read St John's Gospel right through. It's well worth doing; and if you do so, you immediately notice some important differences between St John's Gospel and the other three. In the others, Jesus performs lots of miracles: he restores sight to many blind men, drives out many demons, cleanses many lepers, restores mobility to many paralytics, gives hearing and speech to many who are deaf and dumb.

By contrast, in St John's Gospel, Jesus performs only seven miracles: he turns water into wine at Cana; he cures the son of a courtier; he heals a lame man beside the pool in Jerusalem; he feeds the five thousand; he walks on the lake; he gives sight to a blind man; and he raises Lazarus from the dead. Some of these miracles are described as 'signs'; for example, after Jesus turns the water into wine, St John says, 'This was the first of the signs given by Jesus.' And all seven miracles are clearly signs of something bigger than themselves. The miracle of Jesus giving sight to a man born blind, illustrates a key theme of John, that Jesus is the light of the world. John announces this theme on the very first page of his Gospel: 'That life was the light of men, a light that shines in the dark, a light that darkness could not overpower.' And Jesus, as soon as he encounters this blind man, says, 'As long as I am in the world, I am the light of the world.'

Notice that the man was *born* blind. In the other gospels, Jesus *restores* sight to the blind. But this man has *never* seen. Jesus is not restoring something lost, he is giving something entirely new. And Jesus enlightens not only the man's eyes, but his mind. In fact the man is in every way transformed. To begin with, he is completely passive. Blind Bartimaeus, in St Mark's Gospel, calls out again and again, 'Jesus, Son of David, have mercy on me.' Not so this man. He doesn't seem to know that Jesus is there.

He doesn't ask for anything. It is Jesus who takes the initiative, makes the paste, puts it on his eyes, sends him to wash in the pool. The blind man simply does as he is told.

But we see the man changing under pressure from the authorities. He is no longer blind, and he can see through their shallowness and hypocrisy. He can see well enough that Jesus is a prophet. He can see that Jesus has been sent by God. Now we might want him to go further than that: Isaiah and Jeremiah were prophets, they were sent by God, and so was John the Baptist. Jesus is far greater than any of these. The man doesn't yet know this; his eyes are still only half open. Jesus completes the process when he sees him next: 'Do you believe in the Son of Man?' Clearly he has never heard of the Son of Man. 'Sir,' he says, 'tell me who he is so that I may believe in him.' Jesus says, 'You are looking at him; he is speaking to you.' And the man says, 'Lord, I believe' and worships him. He has been brought, in a few hours, from complete ignorance and passivity, to believing in and worshipping the Son of Man. He has completed a very long journey of faith in a very short time.

Each of us is on that same journey of faith, each of us is being more and more illuminated by the Light of the World. Now St Paul says a curious thing about those who are being illuminated: 'Anything exposed by the light will be illuminated and anything illuminated turns into light.' How are we turned into light? The moon has no light of its own. It is a dark ball of rock. But the sun shines on it, and illuminates it; and the moon in turn illuminates our night. Jesus illuminates us so that we may become light and illuminate others. The blind man, from the moment his eyes are opened, becomes a witness to Jesus and a proclaimer of Jesus. Jesus wants us, like him, to be lights to the world, receiving light from him and giving light to others.

What a challenge Jesus offers to us! We are being illuminated by Christ. There is no shortage of people who are in the darkness of loneliness, depression, sickness, unhappiness, or poverty. Christ calls us to be a light in their darkness. A kind word, a thoughtful action, a generous gift, an understanding gesture, a consoling touch: these are within the capacity of each one of us. By offering one of these to someone, we become the light of the world.

Fifth Sunday of Lent
STONE DEAD

Readings Ezek 37:12-14; Rom 8:8-11; Jn 11:1-45

When Oliver Cromwell was drumming up support for the execution of Charles I, he had a sort of motto or catchphrase: 'Stone dead hath no fellow.' He wanted Charles not just deposed or exiled or imprisoned, leaving open the possibility of a movement to restore him, but stone dead.

I dare say we think we know exactly what we mean by death. Death is the great leveller, the one thing we will all have in common, when our time comes.

In fact though, there are many kinds of death. I may experience a kind of death that you do not; and you may experience all kinds of death that are strangers to me. There was once a bishop who used to visit his priests and look at their bookshelves. He wanted to find the date of the latest book they had bought; to find out, as he put it, when their mind had died. There is such a thing as intellectual death, when a person ceases to think in any effective way.

Our readings show us three kinds of death. The Israelites had been carried off in exile into Babylon. Their royal family was extinct, their temple was destroyed, their land removed from them. They had experienced, if you like, national death, or political death, or cultural death. The things that had given them life and identity as a people no longer existed. They still, as individuals, breathed and ate and drank, but as a nation they were dead. So Ezekiel speaks of national resurrection: 'The Lord says this: I am now going to open your graves; I mean to raise you from your graves, my people.'

Saint Paul speaks of another kind of death: spiritual death, or moral death. The kind of death someone has experienced who cannot please God because of sin. Such a person needs a spiritual resurrection, and that is the resurrection which Paul describes: 'Though your body may be dead it is because of sin, but if Christ is in you then your spirit is life itself because you have been justified; and if the spirit of him who raised Jesus from the dead is living in you, then he who raised Jesus from the dead will give life to your own mortal bodies through his Spirit living in you.'

Lazarus, in the Gospel, has experienced physical death, or, as we might think, real death. His death is not a figure of speech, he is not morally dead or culturally dead or intellectually dead: he is stone dead; as still and cold and lifeless as a stone, and with a stone across the mouth of his tomb. And Jesus restores to him the life of his physical body.

Now we might say that Lazarus's death was the real death, and his resurrection the real resurrection. Cultural death or spiritual death are figures of speech, but stone dead hath no fellow. However, the resurrection of Lazarus is just as much a figure of speech as the others. It's not a real resurrection, merely a stay of execution. He has been restored to life, but one day he will die all over again. The real resurrection is that of Jesus, who having died once, dies no more. Death has no more dominion over him. He lives for evermore in an utterly transformed state.

The resurrection we are offered is not simply a restoration of our physical life; that would be merely a figure of speech for resurrection. What we are offered is a share in Christ's resurrection, and that means a transformation of our spiritual and mental and moral lives, as well as of our physical life. Things will not go on as before. It is hard to imagine what that resurrection will be like; we are after all trying to imagine it with minds that have not yet been resurrected.

But we get a few glimpses of it, here and there; only glimpses, but very reliable glimpses. Saint Paul talks of having been caught up into heaven, and to have heard things that cannot be told, which man may not utter. Nor did he utter them; but with the benefit of that vision he tells us, in another place, 'I consider that the sufferings of this present time are not worth comparing with the glory that is to be revealed to us.'

Passion (Palm) Sunday
SIMON OF CYRENE

Readings Isa 50:4-7; Phil 2:6-11; Mt 26:14–27:66

I've always been interested in Simon of Cyrene. Matthew tells us nothing about him except that he came from Cyrene, which is in north Africa. Mark, who is always better-informed than Matthew, tells us that he was a passer-by, that he had come in from the country, and that he was the father of Alexander and Rufus. Our translation says that they enlisted him to carry the cross, but that is rather weak; other translations say, more accurately, that they *compelled* him to carry that cross. Nobody would volunteer for such a job. He was a passer-by, he was not from those parts, he knew nothing of what was going on, it was not his affair, he was not a follower of Jesus. But he was in the wrong place at the wrong time, so they compelled him to carry the cross. I dare say the episode spoiled his whole day. Not only did he have the effort and inconvenience of carrying a heavy cross through the crowded streets, he didn't even have the consolation of reflecting that he'd helped in a good cause. He'd simply assisted in the execution of a criminal: a distasteful and demeaning task.

So often the crosses imposed on us are like the one imposed on Simon. The times when we've worked hard for a good cause, the times we've gone out of our way to visit the sick, to help the needy: those are not our crosses. Those are our good deeds. Our crosses are the times when we have endured meaningless and unmerited suffering, suffering without any point or purpose or redeeming features whatever; or indeed, the times when we've been prevented from doing our good deeds by futile and frustrating distractions. Simon of Cyrene, no doubt, had better things to do than to carry that cross; he could have put the time to better use, giving alms to the poor, teaching Alexander and Rufus about their faith, doing all manner of good deeds.

For that matter, have you ever thought what Our Lord could have done on that Friday, if he had not been crucified? He could have spent the day healing the sick, giving sight to the blind, raising the dead, proclaiming the word of God. And yet we know that none of the good works which Jesus did could ever equal the worth of his sacrifice on the cross. Nor are any of the good deeds of Simon of Cyrene remembered, except his carrying of the cross.

I've wrestled all my life with trying to understand the meaning of the crucifixion, and I'll no doubt go on wrestling with it till the day I die. But for the moment, it seems to me that the meaning of the crucifixion lies precisely in its meaninglessness. It gives meaning to all the other futile crosses that people are called upon to bear. People whose houses have been burned, or who have been executed, or driven from their homelands in so many troubled parts of the world: what meaning or justice is there in their suffering? None whatever; except that God in Christ has embraced all the futility, all the meaninglessness, all the injustice of human suffering, and claimed it for his own.

Paschal Triduum

Holy Thursday
PASSOVER

Readings Ex 12:1-8.11-14; 1 Cor 11:23-26; Jn 13:1-15

The people of Corinth were irreverent in their manner of celebrating the Eucharist. At that time it was still celebrated as part of a meal, a shared supper. But there was little sharing going on. People were bringing their own food; of course, the rich brought plenty and the poor brought very little. But instead of waiting for the blessing and sharing out their food, they were all tucking into their own food as soon as they arrived, and the poor were going away as hungry as they had arrived. They had all forgotten what Paul had taught them about the Lord's Supper, and so he reminds them: on the night he was betrayed, the Lord Jesus had taken bread, and blessed it, and given it to his disciples saying, 'This is my body;' likewise a cup of wine, saying, 'This is my blood.'

Remarkably, this is the only time in all his letters that Paul ever mentions the Eucharist. Had the people of Corinth not been making such pigs of themselves, Paul might never have had occasion to mention the Eucharist at all, and we might have supposed that he knew nothing about it. Which goes to show how wrong you can be: you can't judge people by what they *don't* say.

For that matter, Saint John never mentions the Eucharist. He mentions a supper which Jesus had with his disciples; but he says nothing of Jesus taking bread and wine, and declaring them to be his body and blood. Instead he describes how Jesus washed his disciples' feet. Again, we might be deceived into thinking that John knew nothing about the eucharist, if it were not taken for granted all through his Gospel: 'I am the bread of life. He who comes to me will never be hungry. He who believes in me will never thirst.' And again, 'If you do not eat the flesh of the Son of Man and drink his blood, you will not have life in you.' And again, 'My flesh is real food and my blood is real drink.' John knew all about the Eucharist, without a doubt.

Then why does he not describe its institution? In a way he does, but not in the way of the other evangelists. John often changes the facts of his story, to bring out their true significance. For example, the other evangelists have Jesus celebrate the Passover with his disciples on the night before he is crucified. His last Passover becomes the first Eucharist. But John has Jesus crucified on the preparation day for the Passover, that is, the eve of the Passover. Why does he do this? So that Jesus is now crucified at the very time the lambs are being slaughtered in the Temple for the Passover. Jesus *is* our Passover lamb who is sacrificed for us. His death *is* the Eucharist, the giving of his body and blood to be our Passover meal.

John takes a few liberties with the facts. But let's not accuse him of telling lies. In real life, Jesus had to do one thing at a time. He couldn't simultaneously be breaking bread and offering his body to be broken on the cross. But John saw that the two events were one and the same in meaning. So if we want to read John's account of the institution of the Eucharist, we must look at his story of the crucifixion. The soldier pierces Jesus's side with a lance, and out flow blood and water: water for Baptism, and blood for the Eucharist. Both sacraments, John is saying, are instituted by Jesus on the cross. This happens to fulfil the words of Scripture, Not one bone of his will be broken; and those words, from the Book of Exodus, describe how to eat the Passover lamb. Or, as St Paul puts it, Christ our Passover has been sacrificed; let us celebrate the feast.

Good Friday
ST JOHN'S PASSION

Readings Isa 52:13–53:12; Heb 4:14-16; 5:7-9; Jn 18:1–19:42

The four evangelists tell substantially the same story of Christ's crucifixion, but each tells it in his own way, and there are some striking differences. Saint Mark gives what is probably the most factual account, the one nearest to what actually happened. He mentions a young man following Jesus who had nothing on but a linen cloth. The soldiers caught hold of him, but he left the cloth in their hands and ran away naked. Nobody could have invented a detail like that; Mark mentions it because it happened. Saint Matthew is concerned to show the tremendous, earth-shattering significance of Christ's crucifixion, and so, according to him, when Christ died the earth quaked, the rocks were split, the tombs opened and the bodies of many rose from the dead. Saint Luke is concerned to show that Christ was innocent of any crime, and so he has Pontius Pilate say, 'I have gone into the matter myself in your presence and found no charge against him.' And when Christ dies, the centurion says, not 'This man was the Son of God' as in Matthew and Mark, but 'This man was innocent.'

What about Saint John, whose version we have just read? The most obvious thing about John's version is that Christ takes control of the situation. He is in command. The other evangelists have Simon of Cyrene carry the cross for Jesus; John insists that Jesus carried his own cross. The other evangelists have Jesus silent before Pilate; according to John, Jesus does most of the talking. *He* questions Pilate, rather than the reverse: 'Do you ask this of your own accord, or have others spoken to you about me?' We get the impression that it is Pilate, and the High Priest, and the guards and soldiers, rather than Jesus, who are on trial. And that is the truth of the matter. The trial of Jesus is actually *our* trial. He is not the criminal, but the judge. As he says earlier in the

Gospel, 'For judgment I came into this world'; or as he says again just before his passion, 'Now is the judgment of this world.'

How shall we plead, Guilty or Not Guilty? There's no fooling this judge. Saint Luke has the men who were holding Jesus blindfold him and ask, "Prophesy! Who is it that struck you?" But the righteous judge cannot be blindfolded, and the evidence is all too plain. We are guilty as charged. The good news is, that our judge has also borne our sentence, he has paid the price for our crime. He says of us, as he said of Lazarus, 'Unbind them, and let them go.' He came, not to condemn us, but to set us free; and if the Son of God sets us free, we shall be free indeed.

The Season of Easter

Easter Vigil
FEASTING AFTER FASTING

Readings
Gen 1:1–2:2; Gen 22:1-18; Ex 14:15–15:1; Isa 54:5-14
Isa 55:1-11; Bar 3:9-15.32–4:4; Ezek 36:16-28
Rom 6:3-11; Mt 28:1-10

'If in union with Christ we have imitated his death,' says Saint Paul, 'We shall also imitate him in his resurrection.' I certainly hope we shall, because we do a pretty good job of imitating his suffering and death. That is, most of us make some attempt to observe Lent, even if we do nothing more heroic than give up chocolate. Many of us come out to the Stations to walk the path of suffering which our Lord himself trod. Many will have made a point of meditating on the Sorrowful Mysteries of the Rosary during this period. Will we be so diligent in entering into the joy of our Lord's resurrection?

I've been reading the book, *Seven Last Words*, by Fr Timothy Radcliffe, a well-known Dominican. He relates how he was asked to preach on those seven last words, the seven things that Jesus is recorded as saying while hanging on the cross. He says, 'I must admit that I hesitated. They appeared to belong to a gloomy spirituality with which I could not easily identify. Of course, the Gospel says that we are to take up our cross daily and follow Christ, but too often this has spilt over into a Christianity that seemed to me to be joyless, life-denying and with even a hint of masochism.' Fr Radcliffe came, of course, to have a different view of those seven last words, otherwise he would hardly have preached those sermons or written that book, but I dare say we can all recognise the kind of spirituality he was talking about.

The Good News is, that we don't need to be gloomy any more. Actually there was never any need to be gloomy. Jesus tells us that even when we are fasting, we should look cheerful.

How much more cheerful we should look, now that the season of fasting is over. To paraphrase Saint Paul a little, if we have imitated Christ in his fasting, let us now imitate him in his feasting. Tonight begins the season of guzzling, the season of Easter eggs and roast lamb and cakes and ale. If that seems self-indulgent, let us remember that Christ's enemies called him a glutton and a wine-bibber; let us remember also that whenever he describes heaven, it is always in terms of a great banquet, with lots of good things to eat and drink. Let us remember the wedding at Cana in Galilee, which he turned into a foretaste of the heavenly banquet by his presence, when he turned huge quantities of water into wine.

Lent lasts forty days, but Easter lasts fifty days, which immediately tells us that we should put more emphasis on feasting than on fasting, on joy than on sorrow, on celebrating than on lamenting. Christ was in the tomb for three days, but having risen from the dead, he lives for ever.

The glory of his resurrection is out of all proportion to the sorrow of his passion, and we should reflect that disproportion in our theology, and more importantly in our lives. We are the Easter people, the people who are called upon to proclaim that Christ is risen, to proclaim that glorious truth, not only with the words on our lips but with the boldness of our faith, with the smiles on our faces, with the joy in our hearts.

Easter Sunday
RESURRECTION

Readings
Acts 10:34.37-43; Col 3:1-4; (1 Cor 5:7-8); Jn 20:1-9

It wasn't the first time that Peter had preached the resurrection. On that Pentecost morning he had stood in the streets of Jerusalem and said, 'God raised this man Jesus to life, and all of us are witnesses to that.' And every day afterwards Peter had used every opportunity to proclaim the resurrection. On one occasion in the Temple, he and John had cured a crippled man in the name of Jesus of Nazareth; and to the crowds which gathered because of the miracle, he had said, 'God raised Jesus from the dead, and to that fact we are the witnesses.' To Annas and Caiaphas and all the members of the high-priestly families Peter had also spoken about 'Jesus Christ the Nazarene, the one you crucified, whom God raised from the dead.'

But all these people had been Jewish; and now, Peter had been commanded in a vision to go and preach the resurrection to a Gentile family. Peter had been most reluctant to obey the vision, but it had been repeated three times, and no doubt Peter felt ashamed to deny Jesus three times all over again. So in obedience to the vision he had gone to the house of Cornelius. He had probably never entered a Gentile's house before. Jewish people did not. Those who had brought Jesus to be judged by Pilate, had not entered the courthouse for fear of being defiled.

So Peter would have entered the house of Cornelius with some trepidation, some foreboding, some distaste. But enter the house he did; and there he proclaimed the Gospel of the Resurrection, the first time that anybody had ever done so to a Gentile.

And several times in the course of his short proclamation he makes the point that this was not some story which he had made up, or had heard from others; he and his companions were witnesses to the events which he described. 'Now I, and those with me, can *witness* to everything he did ... God raised him to life and allowed him to be seen, not by the whole people but only by certain *witnesses* ... Now we *are* those witnesses – we have eaten and drunk with him after his resurrection from the dead – and he has ordered us to proclaim this.'

'We *are* those witnesses' – a very impressive testimony. And we today are the witnesses to the resurrection. We cannot be eyewitnesses in the same literal sense that Peter was. We were not actually there in Jerusalem when he rose from the dead, we did not put our fingers into the holes in his hands and side, we did not have breakfast with him beside the Sea of Galilee. Nevertheless we are the best and only witnesses that Jesus has. *We* have heard the story, *we* have feasted on his risen body of Christ, *we* have lived his risen life, and he has ordered *us* to proclaim his resurrection just as surely as he ordered Peter. There is no body of people other than the Christians who are going to proclaim the Resurrection. Nor is the proclamation of the resurrection some specialised ministry within the Church, reserved to priests or missionaries. It is a dutly which falls on every one of us. We are the Easter People, the people who live the risen life of Christ, the people who bear witness to his Resurrection, the people called to proclaim that Resurrection, to share that Easter Joy, in season and out of season, to those who will accept it and to those who will not. The kingdom of Satan is destroyed, Sin has lost its power, Death has no more dominion, for Christ is risen: Alleluia!

Second Sunday of Easter
LOCKS

Readings Acts 2:42-47; 1 Pet 1:3-9; Jn 20:19-31

One of my priestly duties used to be to act as Catholic Chaplain to a women's prison in my parish. It was what's called an open prison, which means that it operated a quite humane regime. The prisoners lived in rooms which were never locked, and neither was the gate of the prison ever locked. Inmates were allowed out, on certain conditions, and some of them did jobs in the town.

Another of my duties was to visit my parishioners, and indeed to visit all sorts of people who need help. Once I remember visiting all the houses in my street and inviting the occupants to contribute to a well-known charity. I was struck by how many of the doors in the parish were locked, bolted, barred and chained.

From inside one door, locked more securely than Fort Knox, someone called to me to go away – without even looking to see who I was. It seemed to me a sad irony that people found it necessary to lock themselves in far more securely than the state found it necessary to lock up malefactors.

Twice in the Gospel story we see the disciples making prisoners of themselves, because of fear. On the evening of the first day of the week, that would be the first Easter Sunday, the day of the Resurrection, the disciples are in the upper room, with the door locked. The door is locked to keep their enemies out, but it's also keeping the Gospel locked in; and Jesus doesn't care to have his Gospel locked in. So he comes in anyway, despite the locked doors. And he says to his disciples, 'As the Father has sent me, so I send you' – in other words, 'Open those doors and get out there, and proclaim the Good News.'

It is a bad habit of the Church – and not only of the Church, but of all people – to lock doors, to lock ourselves in and other people out. We can perhaps think of people we try to lock out of our lives. Someone, perhaps, with whom we've had a quarrel. Someone we find irritating, someone we find threatening. Many people try very hard to lock God out of their lives. They have no interest in religion, no interest in discussing the Gospel, no patience with any suggestion that there may be a dimension lacking in their lives.

And it is the amiable habit of Jesus to ignore all those locked doors and to come in regardless. I have a picture hanging in my hallway. It is called 'The Light of the World.' It's quite a famous picture; you may have seen it. It shows Jesus, with a lantern in his hand, knocking at a door. It illustrates the text from the Book of Revelation, 'Behold, I stand at the door and knock. If anyone hears my voice and opens the door, then I will enter his house and dine with him, and he with me.' In my picture, the door has no handle on the outside; it can only be opened from within. And evidently it has not been opened in a long time, because there are tall weeds growing outside.

Jesus is knocking gently, with his bare knuckles. One message of the picture is evidently that we should listen very carefully for that quiet knock, that still small voice of Jesus, because we could very easily miss it and then Jesus would go his way. But I think the picture tells only half the truth. There are times when Jesus ignores that locked door and comes in anyway, or perhaps puts his shoulder to the door and wrenches it from its hinges. Because he wants to be inside with us, dwelling in our hearts, making his home in us. And conversely he wants us to be out there with him, knocking on his behalf at the doors of other people's hearts, proclaiming his Good News. As the Easter Gospel tells us, 'Go out into the whole world – that is, don't stay indoors, locked in our own fear, in our own misery, our own isolation, in that prison which we so often construct for ourselves – but open the door, get out into the whole world, and proclaim the Good News to all creation.'

Third Sunday of Easter
EMMAUS

Readings Acts 2:14.20-28; 1 Pet 1:17-21; Lk 24:13-35

The disciples encounter Jesus in three different ways in the course of their journey to Emmaus. One way is a total failure, another is a partial success, and the third a complete success. First of all they meet him on the road, in the guise of a wayfarer; but they do not recognise him. As Luke puts it, something prevented them from recognising him. We don't know exactly what prevented them; perhaps his appearance was changed by his death and resurrection, or perhaps he deliberately disguised himself; or perhaps they failed to recognise him because of their lack of faith. They did not believe in his resurrection, so he was the last person on earth they expected to meet. Whatever the reason, they totally failed to recognise Jesus in the stranger who walked with them on the road.

Then the disciples meet Jesus in the scriptures, as, starting with Moses and going through all the prophets, he explains to them the passages throughout the scriptures that were about himself. In this experience there was evidently some degree of recognition. They remarked afterwards, 'Did not our hearts burn within us as he talked to us on the road and explained the scriptures to us?' Though they still failed to recognise their risen Lord, they realised that something quite extraordinary was going on, and that this was no ordinary wayfarer.

Finally Jesus takes bread and says the blessing, breaks the bread and hands it to them. Now their eyes are opened and they recognise him; but already he has vanished from their sight. They hurry back to Jerusalem and tell the story of how they had recognised him at the breaking of the bread.

May I suggest that the experience of those disciples is also our own? We recognise Jesus readily enough in the breaking of the bread; our difficulty is in recognising him in any other way. We know very well that Jesus is present in the Mass. The priest holds up the broken bread and proclaims, 'This is the Lamb of God, who takes away the sins of the world;' and nobody would contradict him. We love to encounter Jesus in that broken bread, we receive him reverently, we adore his real presence. But just as Jesus quickly vanished at Emmaus, so he seems to vanish as soon as we have made our Communion. When we leave the church, how conscious are we that he is still with us? We have put aside our fears and worries and quarrels to come and meet Jesus; how long is it before those things return to distract us?

The disciples had a partial encounter with Jesus in the Scriptures; and perhaps that is also our experience. Occasionally a passage of the New Testament moves us so much that we think, Surely this is a message for us. Our hearts burn within us. But more often they do not. If we ever dip into the Old Testament, we may be puzzled or simply left cold by much of it. What have the regulations of the Book of Leviticus, or the thoughts of the prophet Obadiah, got to do with Christ? No doubt some parts of the Old Testament are more central than others to the Gospel message; but it is salutary to reflect that Jesus himself insisted that all the scriptures referred in some way to himself. When he explained the scriptures to the disciples on the Emmaus road, he was not talking about St John's Gospel or the Letters of St Paul; these had not yet been written. He was talking about the Books of Moses – Genesis, Exodus, Leviticus, Numbers, Deuteronomy – and the writings of the prophets. Here, he told his disciples, was where he was to be found. And if we have difficulty in finding him there, maybe we need to do a bit more work on understanding the Bible. Maybe, at the least, we need to read more of it, more often.

The disciples had some glimpse of Jesus in the Scriptures, but they failed altogether to recognise him in the stranger who walked beside him. Perhaps this is where we too fail to recognise him. We can recognise him well enough in church, but do we recognise him in our fellow men and women? In the members of our own families? In that tiresome relative, whom we really should visit more often? In the sick, in the lonely? In the stranger? In the person of a different religion from ours? We shouldn't suppose that Christ always presents himself in the guise of a Christian. In short, do we recognise him in our ordinary daily lives, in all the thousands of chance encounters we make? I have an awful feeling that when I meet Christ, he will be the one person I thought I could safely ignore.

Fourth Sunday of Easter
THE GATE

Readings Acts 2:14.36-41; 1 Pet 2:20-25; Jn 10:1-10

'My grandfather was a kind and decent man, but he never went to church. Will he go to heaven?' It's a question I'm often asked. Of course, it may not be the person's grandfather. We have fathers, mothers, brothers and sisters, children and friends who may be very dear to us, but who do not share our faith. Will they be saved? We can broaden the question. There are people of many other religions in the world: Jews, Muslims, Buddhists to name but a few. They are all children of God, created in his image. They try to live good lives. Why should they not be saved? And yet, does Jesus himself not say, 'Nobody comes to the Father, except through me'?

To put the matter another way: when Jesus describes himself as 'the gate of the sheepfold,' how are we to understand him? Is a gate for keeping people out, or for letting people in? We may perhaps think of him as a closed gate, locked against all who are not Christians. Yet he does not talk about keeping people out, but letting people in: 'I am the gate. Anyone who enters through me will be safe: he will go freely in and out and be sure of finding pasture.' It is not the case that there was a broad road leading to heaven, and that God put Jesus there as a gate to keep people out. On the contrary, everything we know about Jesus tells us that he is concerned to open doors, to open locks, to open up for us the way to heaven. I cannot tell whether someone's agnostic grandfather will get into heaven or not; but it is not the purpose of Jesus to keep him out. On the contrary, Jesus died and rose again precisely to let him in.

Notice that Jesus says, 'he will go freely in and out.' Having got *in*, why would anyone want to go *out*? And why would Jesus be the way out? Because we do go out from the church into the world to find pasture. It is in the world that we work and earn our living. It is the job of the Good Shepherd, not only to lead his sheep *into* the fold, but to lead them *out* from it into the pasture. When they are actually in the fold, the sheep do not need a shepherd; they need the shepherd to lead them out into the fresh and green pastures, beside the restful waters, through the valley of darkness. Jesus offers us, not only a way into heaven, but a way into our lives, which may often seem dangerous and threatening. There is an illness called agoraphobia, which causes people to be afraid to go outside; they lock themselves instead into their houses. Fortunately the illness is not common, but all of us from time to time may be fearful of the world outside. The temptation is to retreat into ourselves, to avoid making new friends, to stay with people and places and ideas which we know to be safe, and consequently to do very little to build up the Kingdom of God. Jesus sends us out from the safety of our familiar world to conquer new worlds for him. Dangerous it may be, but our Good Shepherd comes with us, to guide us along the right path, to follow us with goodness and kindness, and to promise us that having conquered, we shall dwell in the Lord's own house for ever and ever.

Fifth Sunday of Easter
PRIESTS

Readings Acts 6:1-7; 1 Pet 2:4-9; Jn 14:1-12

'A large group of priests made their submission to the faith.' Things must have been looking up if the Jewish priests were becoming Christians. The priests were leading members of the Jewish religious establishment. It was they who enacted the rituals of the Jewish religion. It fell to them to offer the sacrifices in the Temple. If they were convinced of the rightness of the Christian Faith, this was a major gain for Christianity. Furthermore, the chief priests had been among the leading opponents of Jesus. Caiaphas, the high priest, was among those who had wanted him dead. If the priests were now becoming followers of Jesus, then the Faith was having great success in winning over the hearts and minds of its former enemies.

I wonder, though, if those priests realised that in becoming Christians, they were doing themselves out of a job. The function of a priest was to offer sacrifice by shedding the blood of bulls or of goats. But those sacrifices were no longer necessary. Christ had offered the one perfect sacrifice by shedding his own blood on the cross. The Letter to the Hebrews makes the point

perfectly clearly: 'But when Christ appeared as a high priest …
he entered once for all into the Holy Place, taking not the blood
of goats and calves but his own blood, thus securing an eternal
redemption … For it is impossible that the blood of bulls and
goats should take away sins.'

Of course, the Letter to the Hebrews had not yet been written,
and probably those priests had not thought the situation through
completely. Actually, nobody had thought it through at this time,
for the great controversy in the early Church was whether or not
it was necessary for a Christian to keep the Jewish Law, including
those relating to sacrifices. Saint Paul argued strongly against
any such necessity, but there were those who disagreed with
him, including, for a while, St Peter himself. The Apostles went
up every day to pray in the Temple, and then broke bread, that
is, celebrated the Eucharist, in their own homes. We might ask
them why they bothered to go up to the Temple. They themselves
were the new Temple and the new priests. St Peter writes to the
early Christians that they are the holy priesthood that offers the
spiritual sacrifices which Jesus Christ has made acceptable to
God; they are living stones making a spiritual house, a Temple
of which Jesus is himself the cornerstone. What need had they
of the old Temple, or of the old priesthood?

It all goes to show that it took some time for the full significance of our faith to sink in, even into the minds of the apostles
who had known Christ and who had witnessed his death and
resurrection. Small wonder if we do not always realise the full
significance of what Jesus has done for us, and what he has made
us. 'You are a chosen race, a royal priesthood, a consecrated
nation, a people set apart to sing the praises of God who called
you out of the darkness into his wonderful light.' Has the full
significance of even one of those phrases sunk in?

Because if it has, I wonder that our numbers are not growing
a lot more rapidly than they are. Who would not want to join a
group which was a royal priesthood, a consecrated nation? If we
really presented ourselves as a people set apart to sing the praises
of God, then might we not expect people to be queueing up to

join us? Can we ask ourselves, very seriously, 'Has the significance of what God has done for us in Christ, really sunk in? Do we truly realise what an excellent thing it is that God should send his Son to die on a cross for us, that he should raise him from the dead, and exalt human flesh to a place at his right hand in heaven, that he should send his Holy Spirit upon us, forgive us our sins, fill us with faith and hope and love? Do we truly realise the dignity with which Christ has endowed us, as children of God and heirs with him of the Kingdom of Heaven? And if we do truly realise all this, why are we not doing more about it?'

Sixth Sunday of Easter
SOLOMON

Readings Acts 8:5-8.14-17; 1 Pet 3:15-18; Jn 14:15-21

King Solomon married seven hundred wives. He also had three hundred concubines. And in case he ever felt the need for a little variety, he also had a large number of slave-girls. One day he happened to fall passionately in love with one of his slave-girls, a maiden by the name of Rosanna. He put Rosanna into his harem, intending to marry her and make her his favourite wife. But as soon as she entered the harem, Rosanna fell ill, and daily grew worse until she was at the point of death.

King Solomon was greatly distressed and issued a decree to all the people of Israel and Judah, sending letters also to the King of Egypt, the King of Syria, the King of Lebanon, the King of the Moabites, the King of the Edomites and the King of the Ammonites. He said, 'If anyone can cure my slave Rosanna I will give him anything he asks, even half my kingdom.'

Many eminent physicians tried to cure Rosanna, but to no avail, and she daily grew worse. At last the prophet Mordecai appeared before King Solomon. He bowed low to the ground and said, 'O King, live for ever!' Then he said, 'If it please Your

Majesty, I can cure your slave Rosanna.' The King said, 'If you can do this, ask what you will, even half my kingdom.' But Mordecai said, 'I ask nothing for my labour, but I must warn you that the cure will be very painful. You might think even death would be preferable to the cure.' Solomon said, 'I would be sorry to see Rosanna suffer more pain, but nevertheless you must cure her.' Mordecai said, 'The pain will not be to Rosanna, Your Majesty, but to yourself. Rosanna does not love you, she loves another. You must let her go and give her her freedom, and allow her to marry the man she loves. Then she *will* recover.'

How hard it is to let people go; to admit that they are not our slaves, but have their own lives, their own interests, their own agendas, which are not ours. How hard, how painful it is, to let our parents, our husbands or wives, be taken from us by death! How hard it is to let our children go, to pursue their own careers, their own ideals, which may be very different from ours! But let them go we must; we cannot keep them, they are not our slaves, they do not belong to us. Only by letting them go can we help them to develop and mature so that one day we can enjoy a very different relationship with them.

How hard it was for the disciples to let Jesus go. They would have liked to keep him with them, to have established his kingdom there and then in their own country, to have continued the old familiar relationship they had built up with him. But this could not be. Jesus had in mind a far different kingdom and a far different relationship from what they were used to – actually a far closer relationship, if they did but know it.

So we find him warning them in advance that he must be taken from them, and that this should not be a matter of sadness, but a matter for rejoicing. We find him saying to them, 'Do not let your hearts be troubled. Trust in God still, and trust in me. There are many rooms in my Father's house; if there were not, I should have told you. I am going now to prepare a place for you, and after I have gone and prepared you a place, I shall return to take you with me.' And again, 'I will not leave you orphans; I *will* come back to you.' And again, 'Do not let your hearts be troubled or afraid. You heard me say: I am going away, and shall return. If you loved me you would have been *glad* to know that I am going to the Father.'

Jesus has ascended into heaven, not to leave us orphans, but to establish a new and deeper relationship with us. Filled with the Holy Spirit whom he has sent, feeding on his risen body in the sacrament he has left us, we participate now in his divine life, we dwell in him and he in us; and we have his promise that he is preparing a place for us in his heavenly home, and he will return to take us there so that we may live and reign with him always, in that kingdom which has no end.

Ascension Day
ASCENSION

Readings Acts 1:1-11; Eph 1:17-23; Mt 28:16-20

'Go, therefore,' says Jesus, 'and make disciples of all the nations.' What an immense, daunting task! We might well resent the fact that Jesus has gone off home to heaven and left us with all the hard work. And yet, Jesus really has done all the hard work himself: the nails, the spear, the crown of thorns, the dying on the cross, the lying in the tomb, the harrowing of Hell, the rising from the dead. These things he has accomplished alone. They are the victory. We could not have done these things ourselves, nor are we asked to do them, only to proclaim that Christ has done them.

Still, our task remains a daunting one. 'Go and make disciples of all the nations.' However will we do it on our own? But of course, we are not on our own. Jesus has not really left us. Though ascended into heaven, he is with us still. 'Know that I am with you always; yes, to the end of time.' He is with us still in the breaking of bread, he is with us wherever two or three are gathered in his name. He has sent the Holy Spirit upon us to empower us. So it's up to us to get on with the job, to be his witnesses to all the ends of the earth.

Seventh Sunday of Easter
SUFFERING

Readings Acts 1:12-14; 1 Pet 4:13-16; Jn 17:1-11

'If you can have some share in the sufferings of Christ, be glad.' It's an extraordinary idea, isn't it, that we should welcome suffering? That is not how most people think about suffering. We commonly think of pain as a curse, perhaps even as a punishment. We ask God to take it away. We pray for the sick, that they may be relieved of their sufferings. When we are in pain, or we know somebody else in pain, we find it hard to believe that there can be any positive value in that pain.

And yet Peter tells us to be glad if we can have some share in the sufferings of Christ. And Paul tells us in one of his letters, 'Now I rejoice in my sufferings for your sake, and in my flesh I complete what is lacking in Christ's afflictions for the sake of his body, the Church.' That may surprise us, not least because it is hard to believe that there is anything lacking in Christ's afflictions. Were Christ's afflictions not sufficient to bring about the salvation of the whole world?

Yes they were, but even so, it is a privilege to share in those sufferings. By doing so we bring the redemptive power of Christ's suffering into our lives and into the lives of those around us. Christ died, once and for all, for all people, everywhere; and yet we still need to baptise people to make that sacrifice effective in their lives, and we still need to offer the sacrifice of the Mass day by day to make his sacrifice effective in the world today. Christ forgave us all on the cross, and yet we still need the sacrament of reconciliation, to make that forgiveness a reality in our own lives.

It is in fact in the nature of a sacrament to make effective today what Christ has done for us in the past. And it may be that suffering is a kind of sacrament. It may be that our sufferings, joined with those of Christ, have a redemptive quality. We read in the prophet Isaiah, 'Ours were the sufferings he bore, ours the sorrows he carried ... On him lies a punishment that brings us peace, and through his wounds we are healed.' We apply those words, rightly, to Christ; yet they also apply to Christ's body, that is, the Church: that is, to us. It may be that our sufferings, if borne in the right spirit, if offered to the Father in union with Christ's sufferings, may avail for the relief of other people's sufferings, for the extension of the Kingdom of God, for the peace and salvation of the world.

I wonder if we do see our sufferings in that light? Suppose, for example, one of us is diagnosed as having cancer, or some other incurable illness. It is easy to see that diagnosis as a defeat, as the triumph of meaningless suffering over life and health and happiness and all that is worthwhile. It is easy to be filled with fear and despair. But suppose we embrace that suffering as our cross, or rather our share of *Christ's* cross, acknowledging the power of the cross to bring light where there is darkness, to bring healing where there is hurt, to bring peace where there is war, to further the salvation of all the world. Is not our suffering then transformed, given a new meaning and a new dignity?

We are not told to seek out suffering; and indeed it is not necessary to go looking for it. It comes to us all in one way and another. When it comes, it may be that others will say of us, in the words of Isaiah, 'We thought of him as someone punished, struck by God, and brought low.' But for us, suffering may be the path to glory, the gateway to heaven.

Pentecost Sunday
DONATELLO

Readings Acts 2:1-11; 1 Cor 12:23-7.12-13

Once upon a time, long ago, in the City of Florence, in Italy, there lived a sculptor called Donatello. Donatello took it into his head to carve a statue, the most beautiful statue that had ever existed. So he sent to the quarry for a large block of marble. The quarrymen, Mario and Giuseppe, worked all day to cut a block of the required size. They got Mario's son, Benito, to help them load it onto a ox-cart. And they drove the ox-cart all the way to Donatello's studio. They knocked on the door and out came Donatello. He took one look at the block of marble and said, 'It won't do. It's not good enough for my statue. It's flawed. You can take it back.'

Mario and Giuseppe were not at all pleased. They had worked all day to cut the block of marble, and now it looked as though they would be out of pocket. What were they going to do? Mario said, 'I know. There's another sculptor who lives just round the corner. Let's offer it to him.' So they went round the corner and knocked at the other sculptor's door. The other sculptor came out. Giuseppe said, 'Can we interest you in a block of marble? We can let you have a good price on it – it's slightly flawed.' The sculptor said, 'I'll take it. It doesn't matter about the flaw. Bring it into my studio.'

The other sculptor's name was Michaelangelo, and from that block of marble he carved his statue of David, the most beautiful statue that has ever existed.

Do you think God is like Donatello, who won't touch us unless we are perfect? Or is he like Michaelangelo, who takes us, flawed, damaged, imperfect as we are, and turns us into his masterpiece?

Today's feast tells us that he is more like Michaelangelo, because the Spirit of God has made his home in us. Poor, cracked, damaged vessels that we are, God's Spirit has made his home in us. He didn't turn his nose up at us because we weren't up to scratch; he made his home in us, and set to work in us, and is even now changing us, transforming us, turning us into his work of art. He didn't refuse to acknowledge us; he has claimed us as his own, paid the price for us, made us his sons and daughters, given us the Spirit that cries out to him, 'Abba, Father.'

Solemnities of the Lord

Trinity Sunday
TRINITY

Readings Ex 34:4-6.8-9; 2 Cor 13:11-13; Jn 3:16-18

Has it ever struck you how much of our Christian faith comes down to us in the form of letters? There are some thirteen letters attributed to St Paul, an anonymous Letter to the Hebrews, a letter of St James, two letters attributed to St Peter, three to St John and one to St Jude. Even that strange book which ends the New Testament, the Apocalypse, or Revelation to St John the Divine, begins with a collection of seven letters to the seven churches of Asia.

Another odd thing is that many of these letters are not letters at all, in the ordinary sense of the word. They are not written to anybody in particular, only as it were to whom it may concern: to anybody who cares to read them. Clearly it occurred to somebody in the early Church – I suspect to St Paul – that if you had something to say about the Christian Faith, it was very convenient to put it down in the form of a letter.

Saint Paul had a great deal to say about the Christian Faith, and he filled every inch of his letters with doctrine. Even at the very end of his letter to the Corinthians, where you or I might be content to write 'Yours sincerely,' Paul crams in a whole book full of teaching: 'The grace of the Lord Jesus Christ, the love of God and the fellowship of the Holy Spirit be with you all.' The 'grace' as we call it, has become very familiar. We use it to close services, or meetings, as a greeting or a blessing. But what a lot Paul says in a few words!

'The grace of our Lord Jesus Christ.' Grace – the whole life of the Christian Church, and of every Christian. God reaching out his hand to help us overcome our sin and weakness, to do everything pleasing to him, to advance on the road to salvation.

The gift of God going before us and following after us, dwelling in our hearts, sanctifying us, strengthening us to do good works, shielding us from evil. And grace, says Paul, is 'of our Lord Jesus Christ.' Like St John, Paul teaches us that grace and truth came through Jesus Christ.

And then Paul goes on, 'The Love of God.' The love of God the Father, whose love made the world, who loved the world so much that he sent his only Son to the the end that all who believe in him should not perish. This is the love which Paul wishes to be with us, and in us, and among us. The love of which St John writes, 'God is love, and he who abides in love abides in him, and he in God.'

And then he writes, 'The Fellowship of the Holy Spirit.' Fellowship – Paul uses a lovely word in his own language, *koinonia*. It can mean fellowship, the sort of fellowship people have with each other, providing care and support and company for each other. It can also mean a contribution, a sharing, as when we share our goods or money with those less well-off than ourselves. Paul would have used the word for the collection we take during the Mass; and it's an interesting thought that he would have used the same word for what we share with God and for what God shares with us, for another meaning of that word *koinonia* is Communion. The Blessed Sacrament, the Body of our Lord Jesus Christ, Paul calls a *koinonia,* that is, a sharing, in God. And that sharing, says Paul, is the gift of the Holy Spirit.

We celebrate the feast of the Most Holy Trinity, of God the Father, God the Son and God the Holy Spirit. It is curious that we should feel the need of a Sunday devoted especially to the Holy Trinity, for it is in the Holy Trinity that we live and move and have our being. We celebrate the Holy Trinity every time we make our prayers to the Father, through Jesus Christ, in the power of the Holy Spirit. We celebrate the Holy Trinity every time we share with one other the grace of our Lord Jesus Christ, and the Love of God, and the Fellowship of the Holy Spirit.

Corpus Christi
THE BODY OF CHRIST

Readings Deut 8:2-3.14-16; 1 Cor 10:16-17; Jn 6:51-58

In the year 1192 a little girl called Juliana was born in a village near Liège, in France. She was orphaned, and and placed in a convent, where she made rapid spiritual progress and began to experience visions. The effect of these visions was to inspire her to agitate for a feast commemorating the institution and gift of the Holy Eucharist. She died in 1258, and her efforts were rewarded posthumously when the feast of Corpus Christi, the Body of Christ, was instituted in 1264.

The obvious time to commemorate the institution of the Holy Eucharist would have been Holy Thursday, but at that time the passion was commemorated on that day, and it was thought best to choose a separate day; and the Thursday after Trinity Sunday was chosen. The leading theologian at the time, Saint Thomas Aquinas, is said to have composed the office for the day. This included the collect with which we began this Mass, and a couple of Eucharistic hymns. Verses from those hymns are used to this day at Benediction, that is to say, the *O Salutaris* and the *Tantum ergo.*

He also wrote a hymn for the Mass of Corpus Christi, the *Lauda Sion Salvatorem,* which, though less well known, is a remarkable work. It expresses in verse much of St Thomas's eucharistic teaching, which he had set forth at length in his books. Almost every line reflects some controversy or debate about the Eucharist which had taken place in the previous hundred years. Let me read you just a couple of lines from that hymn, in an English translation:

> Whoso of this Food partaketh
> Rendeth not the Lord, nor breaketh:
> Christ is whole to all that taste.

This refers to the moment at the Mass when the priest breaks the host into several pieces, what we call the *fraction*. This was originally a purely practical action, done so that each communicant could have a piece. Christ himself broke the bread at the last supper, and gave a piece to Peter, a piece to John, a piece to Andrew and so on. Nowadays we use small individual hosts, and only those near the front of the queue would receive a fragment of the large host; but in principle, everybody receives a small part of the broken host.

The point that Aquinas makes in his hymn is that although the bread is broken, Christ himself is not broken or divided up. However small the particle you receive, you receive the whole Christ. I find that a very moving thought. The most insignificant crumb contains all that God has to offer us, the crucified and risen and ascended body of his Son. And the same is true of the precious blood: the smallest drop contains the whole Christ.

What is more wonderful still is that everyone alike, whether old or young, male or female, famous or obscure, rich or poor, saintly or sinful, receives alike the whole Christ in his or her portion of the sacrament. To you and to me, just as much as to the great saints, Christ gives himself whole and entire. We, just as much as Saint Thomas Aquinas or Saint Francis or the Blessed Virgin herself, receive all Christ has to give, all the grace we need to get to heaven, all the grace we need to perform great works for Christ.

So often we put ourselves down, underestimate what we can do to build up the kingdom of God. If only we had been given the graces that the saints had received, what great things we could do! But we see in this feast how a great festival could be established by an orphan girl, born in an village no-one has heard of and locked away in an obscure convent. It may remind us of a great place of pilgrimage founded in another obscure village in France by another young girl, Saint Bernadette, or of another founded in the tiny English village of Walsingham by the Lady Richeldis; indeed it may remind us of great things done through another girl in an even smaller village called Nazareth. We, like them, can do wonders for God; all the graces given to them are available to us in every crumb of the blessed sacrament, in every drop of the precious blood.

The Ordinary Sundays
of the Year

*The Baptism of Our Lord takes the place of
the First Sunday of the Year.*

Second Sunday of the Year
TO THE ENDS OF THE EARTH

Readings Isa 49:3.5-6; 1 Cor 1:1-3; Jn 1:29-34

The Holy Land is not a very big country. It's about the size of Wales; small in comparison with England, tiny in comparison with its great neighbours, Egypt and Assyria and Babylon. The Israelites were never a very numerous people; their numbers were probably counted in thousands rather than in millions. They were never a very strong people, in comparison with the mighty empires on each side of them. And, getting on for six hundred years before the time of Christ, it looked as though they had been snuffed out altogether. The King of Babylon had invaded their land, destroyed their cities and their temple and massacred many of them. Some of those who escaped the massacre fled as refugees to other countries such as Egypt. Most of the survivors however were carried off in captivity to Babylon, and there they endured seventy years of exile.

Those seventy years, counting from about 587 BC, were the low point in Israel's fortunes. Without their temple, they could not practice the main acts of worship prescribed by their religion. It was as though Catholics were unable to celebrate the Mass. They had no king, no functioning priests, no sacrifice, no reasonable hope of any improvement.

And during this period, God raised up a prophet among them. We don't know his name; usually we refer to him as

'Second Isaiah' because his writings are included in the Book of the Prophet Isaiah. The real Isaiah had lived over a hundred years earlier. And Second Isaiah promised deliverance to the Israelites, a return to their own country. But that was the least of it. To restore the Israelites to their home would be too small a thing for God. He would do something far greater. He would raise up from among them a Servant who would be the light of all the nations, so that God's salvation would reach to the ends of the earth.

You have to be astonished at the confidence, the audacity, of Second Isaiah. His people were crushed, defeated, exiled; hardly a people at all. And yet, said the prophet, they would be the means of bringing God's salvation to the ends of the earth. No half measures there!

We can sometimes get despondent at the fact that Mass attendance seems to be going down, or that we are getting very few vocations to the priesthood. Nobody could maintain that this is the golden age of Christianity in England. And yet things would have to get a great deal worse, a very great deal worse, before they even began to approach the desperate plight of the Israelites in Babylon. Without doubt God can turn around our present difficulties, far more easily than he was able to restore the fortunes of Israel. But what exactly do we want him to do for us? Give us more priests? Encourage more people to come to Mass? He could do these things in the twinkling of an eye. But he has something far greater in mind. He wants to make us the light of the nations, so that his salvation may reach the ends of the earth.

Second Isaiah invited the Israelites to raise their expectations. They were praying, no doubt, to be able to survive the coming day, for some relief from their grinding poverty and oppression; the most optimistic prayed to be allowed to return to their own country and re-establish some kind of national life. All that, said Second Isaiah, is not enough for God. Pray rather, he says, to be made the light of the nations, so that God's salvation may reach the ends of the earth. And he issues the same invitation to us. Don't pray simply that we may have enough priests to say the Mass, or enough resources to keep our churches open. Pray that we may bring God's salvation to the ends of the earth, pray that we may build up on earth his kingdom of justice and peace, pray that the earth may be filled with the glory of God as the waters cover the sea.

Third Sunday of the Year
FISHERS OF MEN

Readings Isa 8:23–9:3; 1 Cor 1:10-13.17; Mt 4:12-23

It used to be said that in the intelligence services, if someone had a degree in Russian, he was put in the Spanish section; if he had a degree in Spanish, he would no doubt he put into the Russian section. Our Lord takes far more care to use the talents of those he calls into his service. He calls the fishermen, Peter and Andrew, James and John, and promises to make them 'Fishers of Men.' Now that may seem like a mere figure of speech, but in fact there are similarities between the way you go about catching fish, and the way you go about catching souls for Christ.

You must understand that there were two different techniques for catching fish in ancient Palestine, employing two different kinds of net. There was the casting-net, or *diktuon*, which is what Peter and Andrew are using, and James and John are mending, in this story. To use a casting-net you had to be quiet and watchful, and it was necessary that the water be calm and undisturbed, so that you could see the fish beneath its surface. When you saw the fish, you cast your net over them and pulled them in.

The other kind of net was the dragnet, or *sagene*, which is mentioned in Matthew's Gospel: 'Again, the kingdom of heaven is like a dragnet which was thrown into the sea and gathered fish of every kind; when it was full, men drew it ashore and sat down and sorted the good into vessels but threw away the bad.'

This is a larger net, dragged behind a boat, probably operated by several men, and catching fish which the fishermen might not actually see until they dragged the net ashore.

The two techniques stand for two kinds of evangelism. The dragnet stands for the sort of large-scale evangelism we might undertake by building a new church, or opening a church school, or organising a parish mission. We're not targetting any particular person, but we hope that quite a lot of people will be caught in that net. The casting-net stands for the more personal and individual evangelism that all of us can practice, without the need for any elaborate plan. We have a friend or family member whom we would like to introduce to the Faith. We do not rush in, casting our net blindly, but we wait quietly, observing that person. When the time is right, we make some approach appropriate the the person's needs. We may ask the person if he or she might like to come to church with us, or would like to come to some talk or course about the faith. Many people have been brought into the Church by such quiet evangelism.

The Church needs both these techniques, and can use men and women skilled in either. For that matter, it can use a whole range of skills. Not all those whom Jesus called were fishermen. Matthew was a tax-gatherer; and it's useful to have people in the Church who know how to handle money. Saint Paul was a tent-maker, and I wonder if that gave him any insight into the nomadic life, for of all the saints, Paul especially rejected a settled life and travelled all over the world proclaiming the Gospel. I wonder if he ever slept in one of his own tents on his missionary journeys? Jesus himself was a carpenter; I love to think of him building his Church as one might build a house, selecting twelve strong pillars to bear its weight. Despite his parables, it isn't recorded that he called a real sower to go out and sow the seed of his word, or a real shepherd to look after his flock. I wonder if the 'seventy-two others' whom he called in addition to the twelve, included people from either of those trades?

But what skills do you have, that you can offer to Christ for the building-up of his Church? The Church is looking more than ever to its lay people to take their rightful place in this work. But this is no new idea; it is as old as the Gospel itself. Saint Peter tells us, 'Each one of you has received a special grace, so, like good stewards responsible for all these different graces of God, put yourself at the service of others. If you are a speaker, speak in words which seem to come from God; if you are a helper, help as though every action was done at god's orders; so that in everything, God may receive the glory, through Jesus Christ, since to him alone belong all glory and power for ever and ever. Amen.'

Fourth Sunday of the Year
WHAT IS FOOLISH

Readings Zeph 2:3; 3:12-13; 1 Cor 1:26-31; Mt 5:1-12

A few days ago I came across a book entitled, *The Hundred Greatest Women of All Time.* The Blessed Virgin Mary came in at no. 10, nine places after Eleanor Rooseveldt. It is a laughable illustration of the difference between human standards and divine ones. Actually, I'm surprised that Mary made it into such a book at all, because by the standards of this world she is not particularly impressive. An obscure young woman, probably illiterate, from a poor village called Nazareth, she did not rise to be a queen or even get elected to her parish council. She performed no great charitable work, like Mother Teresa; she was not as good a singer as the Spice Girls, not as good an actress as Madonna, not as good a politician as Margaret Thatcher. All she did was to give birth to a baby called Jesus, who was subsequently executed as a criminal.

How insignificant her life appears from a human point of view; but how very different it appears from God's viewpoint. Mary is the supreme example of God's choosing what is foolish by human reckoning, in order to shame the wise, of his choosing the weak by human reckoning to shame the strong.

She is the supreme example, but not the only example. None of Jesus's early followers were particularly rich, or powerful, or highly educated, or brave, or morally superior to the general run of men and women. Most of his disciples were fishermen – a skilled profession, but not a learned one. The twelve squabbled about who was the greatest among them, and asked Jesus to bring down fire on those who annoyed them – they were not spiritual or moral giants. Peter, their leader, had to employ a scribe when he wanted to write a letter – he was no scholar. All the disciples ran away when Jesus was arrested – they were not much of an army.

Yet these were the men who turned the world upside down, who confronted kings and converted empires. They did so, not by their own power – they didn't have any – but by the power of Jesus dwelling in them, through his Holy Spirit.

What about you? Are you sufficiently foolish to do great things for God? Are you sufficiently weak? Sufficiently timid? Because, if you are, there is room for you in God's great plan. There is a world to be conquered; not by the sword or the gun, but by the Gospel. Those who are full of their own wealth, their own power, their own worth, have no room in them for God, and will never achieve anything for God. It is only the empty who have that space within them to be filled by God: the poor in spirit, those who are hungry and thirsty, not only for earthly food but for meaning and purpose and direction in their lives; those who feel in them a great gaping void of any greatness or goodness they can call their own.

Perhaps you are such a one; I hope so, because if you are, then yours is the kingdom of heaven.

Fifth Sunday of the Year
HELL

Readings Isa 58:7-10; 1 Cor 2:1-5; Mt 5:13-16

People hanker for the good old days, when a bar of chocolate cost sixpence and priests used to preach hell-fire sermons. They say to me, 'Father, how come we don't hear much about Hell any more?' Well, we hear quite a lot about Hell this morning. Jesus warns us no less than three times how unpleasant it is to be thrown into Hell. If your hand causes you to sin, cut it off: it is better to enter into life with one hand than with two hands to be thrown into Hell. If your foot causes you to sin, cut it off: it is better to enter into life with one foot than with two feet to be thrown into Hell. And if your eye causes you to sin, pluck it out: it is better to enter into life with one eye than with two eyes to be thrown into Hell.

These are not popular sayings, and not commonly preached on these days. But they are sayings of Jesus himself; they are not something the Church has made up. No doubt the Church has from time to time come up with some unpleasant teachings, and some improbable ones, and those things we may take with a pinch of salt. But here we are listening to the words of Jesus himself, and we dare not ignore them.

Perhaps the most difficult thing about Jesus's teaching on Hell is that it lasts for ever. The worm does not die, the fire does not go out. We could the more easily reconcile the idea of Hell with that of a loving God if Hell lasted only for a time, even a very long time. Perhaps some people are so evil that it would take a very long time to burn the evil out of them. Then, after a thousand years, or a million years if need be, they could emerge from the flames, purified and made fit for Heaven. But that is not what Hell is about. It never stops. Long, long after the sinner has learnt his lesson, he is still confined to the flames of Hell, and always will be. His sufferings do not improve him or purify him; they do him no good at all.

Even so, you might say, there may be some who deserve such punishment, perhaps Adolf Hitler or others who engaged in genocide or torture. How could they ever expect to attain the joys of Heaven? But Jesus was not talking to mass murderers. He was talking to farmers and fishermen, shepherds and sowers of seeds, husbandmen and housewives; very ordinary people, just like you and me. Were they in serious danger of Hell fire? Are *we?*

These thoughts disturbed me so much that I did a little reading about Hell. One text-book informed me, 'Modern theology tends to stress the fact that hell is but the logical consequence of ultimate adherence to the soul's own will and rejection of the will of God, which (since God cannot take away free will) necessarily separates the soul from God, and hence from all possibility of happiness.' But I don't believe that God *cannot* take away free will. Nothing is impossible for God. And we ourselves have no excessive regard for free will. If we see our children about to walk in front of a bus, we don't allow them to do so on the grounds that it's *their* choice. We override their free choice, if that choice would be harmful to them or to others.

Actually our whole society, and every conceivable society, is based on putting limits to free will. We make people pay taxes, whether they wish to or not; we confine prisoners in gaol, though given the choice they would surely prefer to be at liberty. We force people to drive at a reasonable speed, to respect other people's property and do a thousand other things which may be quite against their will. Why should God alone be so concerned to respect our free will? And *are* people in Hell there of their own free choice? Surely nobody would give his free and informed consent to spend eternity in Hell. Those who are there didn't believe Hell really existed, or didn't realise it would be that bad, or didn't realise their conduct was quite bad enough to deserve Hell. They did not contemplate Hell in all its horror and all its eternity, and make a deliberate choice to go and live there.

You're all waiting for me to pull a rabbit out of the hat, to tell you the answer to these disturbing questions. You're waiting in vain, I'm afraid, because I don't know the answer myself. But this I do know. We're playing for high stakes. Jesus, through whom, after all, Heaven and Hell and everything else, seen and unseen, were created, assures us that the only sure way to avoid Hell and attain to Heaven is to adhere to his teaching. To ignore it or disobey it will lead to disaster. I don't know exactly what form that disaster will take; and I'd very much rather not find out.

Sixth Sunday of the Year
CUT IT OUT!

Readings Ecclus 15:15-20; 1 Cor 2:6-10; Mt 5:17-37

'If your right eye should cause you to sin, tear it out and throw it away ... and if your right hand should cause you to sin, cut it off and throw it away.' As I don't see too many one-eyed one-armed people in church, I assume that most of us are not keeping these commandments. Nor should we; the Church does not approve of the literal following of these instructions, and condemns those who wilfully mutilate themselves. But if we are not supposed to follow these commandments to the letter, what are we supposed to do? Why do we still read them, if we have no intention of keeping them?

Let's be clear first of all that Jesus talks about cutting our hands off, or plucking our eyes out, only as a last resort if they are preventing us from keeping his other commandments. Now his other commandments, though strict, are not impossible to follow. Aided by God's grace, we can, if we have the will, keep them to the letter. As our first reading says, 'If you wish, you *can* keep the commandments.' It is possible not to be abusive to our brothers and sisters. Sometimes that may involve effort, but we can hardly expect to win the kingdom of God without effort. It is possible to resist the temptations of the flesh, it is possible to avoid taking the Lord's name in vain.

Nowadays we are perhaps a little easy on ourselves with regard to keeping these commandments, and it's salutary to hear our Lord's stern words of warning. From time to time throughout history there have been movements to keep our Lord's commandments more fully and literally. Some, like the Franciscans, have remained within the Church, but have tried to live to the full our Lord's command, 'Go and sell everything you own and give the money to the poor, then come, follow me.' Some, like the Quakers, who strictly observe the commandment not to swear oaths, have left the Church altogether, believing that we have got things hopelessly wrong.

We too can follow our Lord's commands more closely. We may not cut off our hands or pluck out our eyes, but there will be things we do have to cut out, which may be just as painful. We all know that malicious gossip is a sin. Why then is it so often committed? Because we all like to indulge in a little harmless banter. Conversation is one of the great pleasures of life. But when did we last walk away from a conversation, or make an effort to turn it round, when we saw that it was taking an unpleasant turn? It's all too easy to join in with spiteful gossip, much easier than to cut it off. Television is a wonderful source of entertainment, and enlightenment and instruction. Even so, there may be times when it is better to cut it off. That should be a very easy thing to do, since every set is provided with an off switch. Not all those switches are much used. But if we can't take our eyes off a television when it becomes offensive, or turn our ears away from conversation when it turns nasty, it's futile to talk about cutting off our hands or plucking out our eyes.

Seventh Sunday of the Year
LOVE YOUR ENEMIES

Readings Lev 19:1-2.17-18; 1 Cor 3:16-23; Mt 5:38-48

'You have learnt how it was said: you must love your neighbour and hate your enemy.' Where would they have learnt such a thing? Not in the Bible. They would have found in Leviticus the command, 'You must love your neighbour as yourself'; but neither there nor anywhere else in the Old Testament is there a command to hate your enemy. This is human teaching, not the command of God. Jesus often told his listeners that he had not come to abolish the law or the prophets, but to complete them. If there had been a command to hate your enemy, it would have been necessary for Jesus to abolish it; but there is no such command.

The command about taking an eye for an eye and a tooth for a tooth *is* found in the Old Testament, actually in that same book of Leviticus. But its purpose is not to encourage vengeance; rather, it is to set a limit to vengeance. If someone knocks out your tooth, you may knock out his tooth, but you may not kill him. The punishment must be in proportion to the crime, and no greater than the occasion requires. And the Book of Leviticus itself mitigates its own commandment when it says, 'You must not exact vengeance, nor must you bear a grudge against the children of your people.'

Jesus does not abolish the commandments, but he completes them by showing their true scope, and the spirit in which we should keep them. Leviticus tells us to love our neighbour as ourself, but Jesus spells out just what it means to love our neighbour, ultimately by dying for his neighbour on the cross. Jesus teaches us also, who is our neighbour. Not only the person next door, not only the person of the same nationality or religion or race as ourself, but anyone in need of a neighbour.

Jesus brings us back to a true understanding of God's commandments; and to understand God's commandments is to understand God. What sort of a God do we have? Is he a cruel, vengeful God, angry with those who offend him? No, he is a loving God, a God who showers his goodness into the lap of the deserving and undeserving alike. A God who loves his enemies; a God who sends his Son to die for them.

Eighth Sunday of the Year
SOLOMON IN ALL HIS GLORY

Readings Isa 49:14-15; 1 Cor 4:1-5; Mt 6:24-34

Today hardly ever happens. That is to say, the eighth Sunday in ordinary time hardly ever occurs, because it is so often replaced by Trinity Sunday or some other feast. Which is a pity, because on this day we are presented with some of our Lord,s most characteristic and important teaching. We cannot, he tells us, serve two masters; we cannot be the slave both of God and of money. It would be worth revising our lectionary for this reason alone, to bring this great truth more often to our attention, for so many who count themselves servants of the living God are also slaves to the great god Mammon.

And that is not the only great truth concealed by the rarity of this Sunday. Jesus tells us not to worry about our life, and what we are to eat, and what we are to wear. But worry is the great plague of our modern lifestyle. Have a glance at any magazine, and you will see that it is aimed precisely at those who worry about what they eat, and what they wear. It is very disturbing to consider the great gulf that is fixed between the lifestyle which Jesus advocates, with its freedom from worry about money and food and clothing, and the lifestyle which most of us do in fact lead. Is the Church so embarrassed by the disparity that it tucks away Christ's teaching on the subject in the readings for a Sunday which hardly ever happens?

The way out of this unsatisfactory situation, I would suggest, is not to add to our worries by worrying about the way we are failing to lead the Christian life; that would hardly be the way to obey Christ,s command not to worry. The best plan is the one which Christ himself advocates: to consider the lilies of the field. Let us spend more time in our gardens, or in the country, looking at the wonders of nature, admiring the beauty with which God has clothed the fields. There is a very well-trodden road leading from admiration of the beauties of nature, to adoration of the Father of all beauties. There is a profound spirituality in the simple words of the well-known children's hymn by Mrs C. F. Alexander:

> All things bright and beautiful,
> All creatures great and small;
> All things wise and wonderful,
> The Lord God made them all.

The same road has been trodden by one of the greatest of spiritual masters, Saint Francis, in his *Canticle of Brother Sun*: 'Be praised, my Lord, for sister moon and the stars, in heaven you have made them clear and precious and lovely. Be praised, my Lord, for brother wind and for the air, cloudy and fair and in all weathers – by which you give sustenance to your creatures. Be praised, my Lord, for sister water, who is very useful and humble and rare and chaste ... Be praised, my Lord, for sister our mother earth, who maintains and governs us and puts forth different fruits with coloured flowers and grass.'

Neither Saint Francis, nor Mrs Alexander, nor indeed Jesus himself, suggests that the created world is evil or unworthy of admiration. On the contrary, it is good, it is very good, because God has created it and has declared it to be very good. But if the creation is good, how much more excellent is the creator, and if he can endow even the inanimate parts of his creation with such beauty, how wonderfully he will provide for the human race, which he has made in his own image, and redeemed with the blood of his Son. Therefore let us not worry about tomorrow, or about anything else, but let us set our hearts on his kingdom, and on his righteousness, confident that all we need will be given to us by God, our maker and redeemer, our Father and our friend.

Ninth Sunday of the Year
BUILDING A HOUSE

Readings Deut 11:18.26-28; Rom 3:21.25.28; Mt 7:21-27

Anyone who listens to the words of Jesus and acts on them will be like a wise man who built his house on a rock; and anyone who listens to the words of Jesus and does not act on them will be like a foolish man who built his house on sand. But what does it mean to build a house? Surely to build a house is to build our-self, to build up our character and personality from the building blocks available to us. We do in a very real sense build our own personalities, we are not just born with them.

This is more obvious if we consider the case of the foolish man who built his house on sand. Imagine a young man, a boy if you will. He has the same advantages of health and education and natural ability as anyone else, but he begins to make poor choices. He hangs around with bad company, he neglects his work, he selects superficial goals in life. Before long he's in trouble with the law, he's unemployed and unemployable. Nobody made him that way: he chose to build his house on sand, and the inevitable consequence is, that house will one day fall.

Consider now the man who built his house on a rock. His choices are governed by the principles of the Gospel. God sets before each of us, as he set before the Israelites, a blessing and a curse. This man chooses the blessing. In his dealings with others, he remembers the saying of Jesus, 'Blessed are the merciful: they shall have mercy shown them.' And so he does not seek revenge on those who annoy him, he does not act spitefully. In his attitude to the world he remembers the words of Jesus, 'Blessed are those who hunger and thirst for what is right'; and so he seeks to act justly, and to desire justice for others. This affects how he does business, how he votes, what charities he supports, and a thousand other matters. When conflicts arise in his family life, or at work, or in his circle of friends, he remembers the words of Jesus, 'Blessed are the peacemakers;' he works for the peace of all, and so he does not tell tales or bear grudges. Often he will swallow an insult rather than react to it.

He remembers that he is called to be the salt of the earth, and strives not to grow stale or insipid, but to impart a wholesome flavour to whatever he touches. He remembers that he is called to be the light of the world, and tries to let his light shine in the sight of men, so that they may see his good works, and glorify his father in heaven. To those who seek his aid, he gives generously, but not ostentatiously: his right hand does not know what his left hand is doing. He is at pains to store up treasure, not on earth but in heaven, and that is where his heart is fixed. He does not worry about tomorrow, having enough faith to believe that God will provide for his needs. He does not judge others, knowing that the judgement he gives will be the judgement he receives. He prays about everything.

Every choice he makes not only makes the world around him a better place, but it builds up the house of his soul, builds it up firmly and securely on a rock. That house will not be built in a day, it will be built up over many years, built up of many thousands of bricks, each brick a right choice, cemented together by sound principles. That house will not fall, it will stand. It will stand, not only in this life, but in the life to come, through all eternity.

Tenth Sunday of the Year
FOLLOW ME

Readings Hos 6:3-6; Rom 4:18-25; Mt 9:9-13

'Follow me' said Jesus to Matthew; and Matthew immediately got up and followed him. And down through the centuries, Jesus has continued to say to people, 'Follow me' and they have continued to get up and follow him. I dare say that each of us has heard that call and got up and followed Jesus. Or have we? It may be that some people are brought to church by their parents, and come because they have to, and perhaps continue to come out of habit, but have never really heard that call, never been convinced of the truth of the Gospel, never made a conscious decision to get up and follow Jesus.

If you are one such person, let me, in the name of Jesus, issue to you that personal challenge: 'Follow me.' Why? Why should we follow Jesus? As good an answer as any is provided in the Preface to today's Mass: 'Through his cross and resurrection he freed us from sin and death and called us to the glory that has made us a chosen race, a royal priesthood, a holy nation, a people set apart.'

'Through his cross.' Jesus has shown his love for us by dying for us. Saint Paul writes somewhere, 'It is not easy to die even for a good man – though of course for someone really worthy, a man might be prepared to die – but what proves that God loves us is that Christ died for us while we were still sinners.'

'And through his resurrection.' Others have died, many have died heroic and sacrificial deaths. Christ alone has risen from the dead, and shown himself to be someone of a different order from any of those others who have died, someone with power over death itself. Again, Saint Paul says, 'He abolished death, and he has proclaimed life and immortality through the Good News.'

Our Preface continues 'He has freed us from sin and death' condensing what Saint Paul says: 'The law of the spirit of life in

Christ Jesus has set you free from the law of sin and death.' and it goes on to quote from the words of Saint Peter: 'You are a chosen race, a royal priesthood, a consecrated nation, a people set apart to sing the praises of God who called you out of darkness into his wonderful light.'

'A chosen race' – chosen and called by God, a race not by virtue of physical characteristics or skin colour, but by virtue of our common baptism into Christ; a royal priesthood, royal by virtue of belonging to Jesus our Lord and King, a priesthood called to share in the work of Jesus in sanctifying the whole of creation. A people set apart to sing the praises of God who has called us out of the darkness of doubt, out of the darkness of guilt and anxiety, out of the darkness of fear, into the wonderful light of his gospel, the light of joy and peace and glory.

Those are the claims Jesus has on us, and why we should get up and follow him. I don't know how much of this Matthew realised when he got up and followed Jesus. Perhaps all he understood was that his present life, as a tax-gatherer and collaborator with the Roman, was contemptible, something of which he was ashamed, and this man Jesus offered a way of life which might restore his self-respect. For that matter I don't know how much of the Gospel message we ourselves can take in, and how much is mere talk. To talk of being called out of darkness into God's wonderful light may not mean very much to us, unless perhaps we find ourselves plunged into the darkness of a deep depression, or some fearful situation from which we cannot imagine any way of escape, and then we find Jesus knocking at our door and calling us out into his wonderful light.

Whatever we are missing in our lives and want to obtain, whether it is self-respect, the assurance of forgiveness, an honourable purpose in this life or the hope of a life to come, we shall find it if we follow Jesus, who invites us in these gracious words: 'Come to me, all you who labour and are overburdened, and I will give you rest. Shoulder my yoke and learn from me, for I am gentle and humble in heart, and you will find rest for your souls.'

Eleventh Sunday of the Year
THE GOOD SHEPHERD

Readings Ex 19:2-6; Rom 5:6-11; Mt 9:36–10:8

Jesus took pity on the crowd because they were harassed and dejected, like sheep without a shepherd. I wonder if you ever feel harassed and dejected, like a sheep without a shepherd? So often we fall prey to anxiety, to stress, to doubt, to worry, to depression. Probably very few people escape such feelings. And these feelings tell us that nobody loves us, that nobody cares for us, that we are alone, that we don't matter very much, that nobody would notice if we died.

And yet the most important thing our religion tells us is that this is not so. We are loved, we are cared for. God loved the world so much, that he sent his Son to give his life for us. Actually, let's forget about the world for a moment. The world is a big place, and we can get lost in it. God loved us, you and me, so much, that he sent his Son to give his life for us. And his Son is risen, and lives to be our good shepherd: the one who cares passionately when we are in danger, or in grief, or in perplexity or doubt or distress. The shepherd who puts himself out to fetch us back from the wilderness in which we get ourselves lost.

You'd think this would be well known. After all, 'The Lord is my shepherd' is the most familiar of all the psalms; I remember learning it by heart at primary school. Many people have it on a plaque on their wall.

And our Lord so often, in his teaching, in his parables, presents himself as the Good Shepherd: 'I am the good shepherd, and I know my sheep … If a man has a hundred sheep, and one of them has gone astray, does he not leave the ninety-nine on the hills and go in search of the one that went astray?'

And yet this familiar and basic teaching often gets forgotten, if indeed it is ever properly learnt. So many people could enumer-ate the seven sacraments, or the ten commandments, or recite the catechism, or tell you what are the holy days of obligation, or any of the other rules and regulations of the Church, but haven't learnt this basic truth by heart: that God loves us, that he cares for us, that he never forgets us or abandons us to our own devices. Even when things look bad, when our loved ones fall ill or are taken from us, when we fall into difficulties or disgrace, when we walk, as the psalm says, 'in the valley of darkness' – or as an older translation put it, more vividly, 'through the valley of the shadow of death' – we still need fear no evil; the Good Shepherd is there with his crook and his staff to give us comfort. Surely, with such a good shepherd, goodness and kindness shall follow us all the days of our life, and we shall dwell in the Lord's own house for ever and ever.

Twelfth Sunday of the Year
THE VIRUS

Readings Jer 20:10-13; Rom 5:12-15; Mt 10:26-33

We hear a lot nowadays about computer viruses. I wonder if you know what that means? It means that some joker devises a programme which gets into your computer and does nasty things to it, perhaps destroying all the data in your computer. It spreads from computer to computer because most computers are connected by telephone cable. You receive, over the internet, what purports to be an innocent message from a friend. It is in fact a set of instructions telling your computer to self-destruct, but not before it has sent out similar instructions to many more computers, rather like chain-letter. It's called a virus because it acts like a virus. You catch, say, the flu virus from another person, and it devastates your system, and also is passed on to other people, devastating them in turn.

Saint Paul writes as though sin and death were viruses. 'Sin entered the world through one man, and through sin death, and thus death has spread through the whole human race.' Sin does indeed act like a virus. We see that in so many conflicts in the world. Violence breeds violence, brutality begets brutality. Those who have been tortured seldom learn from the experience how to be kind and gentle to others; rather, they learn to torture in turn.

We see the same thing in family relationships. So often those in our prisons have been abused as children, either sexually or physically or mentally. These children deserve, and usually get, our sympathy. But too often when they grow up they in their turn become abusers, passing on the lessons they learned in childhood. Evil is like a virus, being passed on down the generations. Obviously what is needed is for somebody to call a halt, somebody to refuse to pass on that virus. We see such a refusal in the case of Our Lord. Hanging on the cross, bearing the weight of all the accumulated evil of the world, he calls a halt. He says to his father, 'Let all this suffering, all this violence, all this evil, end right here with me. Don't pay them back in their own coin, don't punish them, don't lay this sin to their charge. Father, forgive them.'

We can do the same, in our own lives. We can refuse to pass on the virus, refuse to pay others back as they have paid us. We can decline the opportunity to strike the cheek of those who strike ours. We can absorb the evil and not pass it on. We can say, 'Forgive us our trespasses, as we forgive those who trespass against us.' And indeed if we don't, we have little claim to be Christians, because that is the great lesson which Christ teaches.

But Saint Paul writes of another sort of virus. 'If it is certain that through one man's fall so many died, it is even more certain that divine grace, coming through the one man, Jesus Christ, came to so many as an abundant free gift.' Grace too spreads through the world like a virus, originating in Jesus Christ and passed on from person to person by a kind word, a friendly smile, a helpful action. And this is a virus that we very much want to pass on. With this particular virus let us be as careless and unhygienic as we can be. Let us seek out every contact that serves to contaminate others with this virus of God's grace, God's love, God's saving help, God's forgiveness, God's wonderful gift of salvation through our Lord Jesus Christ.

Thirteenth Sunday of the Year
ALL CREATURES GREAT AND SMALL

Readings
2 Kgs 4:8-11; 14-16; Rom 6:3-4.8-11; Mt 10: 37-42

We like to think that our religion favours the family. After all, one of the Ten Commandments is, 'Honour your father and your mother.' In the Catholic Church, we regard marriage as a sacrament, and binding for life. We attach great importance to the care and upbringing of our children. And so it's a shock to find Jesus apparently making light of family relationships: 'Anyone who prefers father or mother to me is not worthy of me. Anyone who prefers son or daughter to me is not worthy of me.' No doubt we should love God more than we love any of his creatures; but does Jesus have to put the matter quite so bluntly?

Actually I've given away the whole substance of my homily in that last sentence. Let me repeat it: No doubt we should love God more than we love any of his creatures, but does Jesus have to put the matter quite so bluntly?

Let's take the second part first: does Jesus have to put the matter quite so bluntly? Yes, I'm afraid it is the habit of Jesus to put everything bluntly. If he'd been a bit more tactful, they wouldn't have crucified him. We preachers think twice about what we say, we try to avoid giving offence or hurting people's feelings. The words of Jesus come straight from the heart of God and they are not watered down with tact or prudence. From Jesus we get the pure word of God, neither tarnished nor polished. If we don't like it, that's too bad.

But to the first part of my sentence: no doubt we should love

God more than we love his creatures. Of course we love his creatures, and so we should. We love our mothers and fathers, our wives and husbands, our children, and indeed all people: our friends, our neighbours, the stranger, those of a different race, or colour, or religion than ourselves. We should love them all. And not only people: we love, or we should love, all creatures great and small. A remarkable hymn, actually, that one: 'All Things Bright and Beautiful, All Creatures Great and Small.' The hymn lists all the wonders of nature: each little flower that opens, each little bird that sings, the purple-headed mountain, the river running by, the sunset and the morning. We should love them all, not just because they strike us as beautiful, but because God has made them, and when he made them, he saw that they were good, they were very good.

But we must not love the creatures more than we love the creator. I recently stayed in one of our English monasteries. This monastery has one of the most beautiful churches in England, a joy and an inspiration to worship in. The monastery is not doing too well at the moment for numbers. They are not getting any novices, the community is dwindling. I had an awful feeling as I looked around their church that one day, perhaps in the not-too-distant future, it may close. That, I thought, would be a disaster; we should do everything in our power to keep it open. But should we? If we lavish all our love and care on the building, we make it into an idol. If we lavish all our love and care on God, he will provide us with a building in which to worship him.

Indeed he has already done so, by giving us the new temple, Jesus Christ. Recently I visited Jerusalem, and saw all that remains of the old temple. There's just one wall standing, and the Jews go there to bewail the loss of their beautiful and holy temple. But as Christians, we have nothing to wail about. God has given us a new temple, a temple not build with hands, our Lord Jesus Christ.

And that new temple is eternal. It will never close, or be torn down. One day all the created universe will be taken from us. We fear to lose our parents, or our husbands and wives, or our children. But sooner or later we shall lose them all. We shall lose our faculties, our bodies, the very breath of life. All will one day be taken from us. One thing will not be taken from us: the salvation given to us in our Lord Jesus Christ, the new and everlasting temple, the only Son of the Father, who will raise us up to be with him in glory, to gaze forever on the infinite beauty of the creator, and to tell how great is God Almighty, who has made all things well.

Fourteenth Sunday of the Year
GENTLE

Readings Zech 9:9-10; Rom 8:9.11-13; Mt 11:25-30

Our First Reading is a bit of a puzzle. 'See now, your king comes to you; he is victorious, he is triumphant, humble and riding on a donkey, on a colt, the foal of a donkey.' That reading would be very appropriate on Palm Sunday, when we think about Jesus riding into Jerusalem on a donkey; but what does it have to do with today?

The point we have to take up today is not that Jesus rode on a donkey, but that he is humble, as he says himself in the Gospel: 'I am gentle and humble in heart.' Although he is a victorious and triumphant king, and his empire will stretch from sea to sea, the kingdom he inaugurates is one of peace: he will proclaim peace for the nations, and the bow of war will be banished. A conqueror is not usually humble in heart; a certain arrogance tends to go with the territory. And the burden he imposes is generally heavy. He imposes the yoke of slavery on his conquered subjects, and makes them carry heavy burdens. If Adolf Hitler had conquered this country, I do not think we would have found him humble in heart, and I think we would have found his yoke hard and his burden heavy. But Jesus says, 'My yoke is easy and my burden light.'

Let's look again at what Jesus says: 'Come to me, all you who labour and are overburdened, and I will give you rest. Shoulder my yoke and learn from me, for I am gentle and humble in heart, and you will find rest for your souls.' What Jesus proposes sounds very pleasant, something to be enjoyed. Do you actually enjoy your religion? Do you find it a pleasant thing to come to Mass, do you find it delightful to study the words of Jesus? I think we should. If we come to Mass merely to fulfil a duty, then we're missing something. If we find our religious obligations burdensome, then we've gone wrong somewhere, because Jesus promised they wouldn't be: 'My yoke is easy and my burden light.'

May I propose, as a little exercise for homework, that you spend a few minutes during the week thinking about what you enjoy most in your religion. Perhaps it's the music. It's quite a thought that much of the greatest music ever composed has been written to accompany Catholic worship. Palestrina, Byrd, Haydn, Mozart: it's a wonderful tradition. Or again, much of the finest painting and sculpture the world has ever seen, has been painted or carved to adorn Catholic churches. Think of Michaelangelo's ceiling to the Sistine Chapel, or thousands of lesser but still beautiful works of art that adorn so many of our churches.

Or perhaps you enjoy – and indeed we should enjoy – putting our religion into practice. Coming to the aid of the needy, as we do when we give to CAFOD or Trócaire or Aid to the Church in Need or Let the Children Live! or any of the other charities we support. It should be a source of pleasure to us that there are people who are alive, people who are enjoying reasonable health and standards of living, people who are receiving a decent education, because we care enough to offer them support. To give to such causes is not a burden, or if it is, it's a very light burden.

It pales into insignificance when we think of the great burden that Jesus has borne for us, the weight of our sins and of those of all the world; or when we think of the yoke that Jesus has shouldered for us, the yoke of the cross. He has borne the hard yoke and the heavy burden, so that we might find rest for our souls.

Fifteenth Sunday of the Year
SUCCESS

Readings Isa 55:10-11; Rom 8:18-23; Mt 13:1-23

We have a saying, 'If at first you don't succeed, try, try again.' A very good rule for human beings, because human beings very often do not succeed at the first attempt. But God is almighty; he can do anything he chooses; we cannot suppose that he fails in anything he attempts. As he says through the mouth of the prophet, 'The word that goes from my mouth does not return to me … without succeeding in what it was sent to do.'

Too often though we suppose that God is subject to failure. We say, for example, 'Perhaps God is trying to tell me something.' Now if God really does want to tell us something, he will certainly succeed. Even you and I can tell people something, if we wish. The milkman asks me how many pints I want, and I tell him, two pints please. If I didn't possess the power of speech, I might have to hold up two fingers, or stamp my foot twice. But as it is, I can easily tell him what I want; there is no difficulty in the matter.

A dog or a cat does not possess the power of speech, and sometimes when a dog barks, we say, 'I think the dog is trying to tell us something.' Perhaps there's a burglar, or perhaps the dog is hungry, or wants to go out. The dumb animal cannot make its meaning clear. So often we think of God as a dumb animal, rather than as the one who made the tongue and the other organs of speech, and could perfectly well speak to us in plain language, if he so chose. If God chooses to conceal his meaning from us, he has a reason.

Saint Paul tells us something very similar. The world is a very imperfect place, full of suffering, subject to decay, unable to obtain its purposes. This is not some design fault. God made it that way. If the world is imperfect, it is because it is not yet finished. Saint Paul compares the world with a woman in the act of giving birth. I have to say that I've never given birth myself; it's something I've never tried. But I have been present at a birth, and I've seen how painful and how prolonged it can be. If a visitor from Mars were to pay a five minute visit to earth, and his visit happened to coincide with a woman being in the pangs of labour, he might return to Mars thinking that life on earth was pretty painful. But if he were able to stay awhile and see the birth itself, and the new child, and the joy of the new mother, her former pains forgotten; then he might conclude that life on earth was rather wonderful.

We haven't yet seen the birth of God's new creation, says St Paul. From the beginning till now the entire creation has been groaning in one great act of giving birth. If you thought that this state of affairs was all that there is to God's plan, you would think that the universe was a troubled, unsettled, unstable and rather unpleasant place, and that God must be a very amateurish creator to have made such a botched job of it. But we haven't yet seen the fruits of all God's labour. To use Jesus's own parable, we are witnessing the sowing of the seed, but we haven't yet seen the harvest. We see the seeds being eaten by birds or choked by thorns, but we don't yet see them growing to maturity. In our own lives, we see our troubles, our pains, our failures, our disappointments, but we don't yet see them being taken up into God's plan and transformed into something wonderful.

Our failure to discern the wonder of God's plan is demonstrated nowhere more clearly than in the crucifixion of our Lord. Jesus was arrested, humiliated, tortured and put to death. God's plan for him, to all outward appearances, had ended in failure. As Cleopas said, 'We had hoped that he was the one to redeem Israel.' That was Cleopas's hope; actually a totally inadequate understanding of God's plan. The resurrection showed that the crucifixion was not a disaster but a triumph, not a defeat but the final victory, of significance not only for Israel but for the whole universe.

I wonder what God's plans are for you? What does he have lined up for you? Not only for this life, but for the life to come, that life whose birth-pangs we now witness. How will he use your talents in the creation of new worlds? What wonders God has done already; and yet how much more wonderful is the work he still has in mind, the work in which he calls you and me to be his helpers, and to sow the seeds of his glory!

Sixteenth Sunday of the Year
DARNEL

Readings Wis 12:13.16-19; Rom 8:26-27; Mt 13:24-43

When our society is afflicted with terrorist bombings, our first thoughts are, quite rightly, with the victims; with those killed and injured, and with their families and friends. A week or two down the line, and we can also begin to think about the people who committed those atrocities, and especially about their families and friends, who, perhaps, never suspected that they were terrorists. Can we spare a thought for parents who suddenly discovered that their sons were murderers, for women who discovered that their husbands were terrorists, for children who discovered that their fathers were responsible for a most hideous crime? Those people will have to deal with those terrible revelations as best they can, but how would we react, how would we feel, if the terrorists were members of our own community?

For that matter, how *do* we react when people we know, perhaps members of our own Church, commit deeds unworthy of their religion? Of course, we all do that, as we discover every time we examine our consciences; but some do it more grossly than others. How do we react, for example, when a priest is convicted of abusing a child – something which has happened all too often in recent years. Or when a Catholic is sent to prison for something which is plainly against the commandments of God and the laws of the nation? Perhaps our first reaction is that such people should be thrown out of our Church and no longer regarded as Catholics. Often people outside the Church feel that we should act in just such a way. When the troubles in Northern Ireland were at their height, there were many demands that the Catholic Church should excommunicate members of the IRA.

However, Our Lord in today's Gospel tells us that we should not be hasty in casting anyone out. He tells of a man who sowed good seed in his field. It bears fruit: the wheat grows and ripens. But in the meantime his enemy has sown weeds among the crop. These weeds, the darnel, are the evil people who find their way into the Church: the child abusers, the criminals, the terrorists. The servants suggest that these be plucked out and disposed of, but the Lord commands that they be left where they are for the moment. A lot of harm may be done by a witch hunt. Innocent people may be falsely accused. People who, though sinful, are still capable of amendment, may be denied the opportunity of repentance. There *will* be a reckoning for the wicked, but the Son of Man, not we ourselves, will be their judge. In the meanwhile, we must tolerate their presence among us.

And, as our Lord himself said, it is not the healthy, but the sick, who need a doctor. If someone has a diseased body, the best place for that person is in hospital. But if someone has a diseased soul, where better for that person to be than in the Church? Here are proclaimed the healing and converting words of our Saviour; here is the sacrament of reconciliation, here are all the channels of grace. Sometimes I encounter people who dare not come to Church, because they are so conscious of their own unworthiness. I would say to them, this is the best place for you to be: how do you propose to become *less* unworthy, cut off from the ministry and the sacraments of the Church?

Seventeenth Sunday of the Year
THE KINGDOM

Readings 1 Kgs 3:5.7-12; Rom 8:28-30; Mt 13:44-52

In today's Gospel are two little stories, scarcely long enough to be called parables. The first tells us that the kingdom of heaven is like treasure hidden in a field which someone has found; he hides it again, goes off happy, sells everything he owns and buys the field. The second is rather similar; the kingdom of heaven is like a merchant looking for fine pearls; when he finds one of great value he goes and sells everything he owns and buys it. Both stories are about someone finding something of immense value, so valuable that they each sell off everything they have and buy it. In each case this thing of immense value is the kingdom of heaven.

There is, though, a slight difference between the two stories. The man who finds treasure in a field does so by accident. Perhaps he's been looking for something else. Perhaps he's been ploughing the field, or digging a well. And to his great surprise he has discovered a treasure.

And perhaps there are people who have discovered the Kingdom of God, apparently by accident. Perhaps you are such a person. Perhaps someone has invited you to church. You've come along, perhaps for company's sake, not expecting very much to happen. You've often been to church services before, without being very much moved. But something in the service has touched you deeply. Perhaps it was a very apt scripture reading, or a well-composed homily; or perhaps it was a beautiful hymn, or a comforting word from a member of the congregation. Whatever it was, you realised that you'd found something special, something that matters, something that from now on would be the most important thing in your life.

In the second story, a merchant is looking for fine pearls. He doesn't find them by accident; he seeks them out. He visits markets where fine pearls are sold. He picks up each one in turn, he holds it up to the light, he examines it carefully. If it has a flaw, he puts it aside. Some days he buys no pearls at all. But then he finds the perfect pearl, the one of great value.

He represents the person who is actively seeking God; or at least, is actively seeking meaning and purpose in life. I've met a lot of such people. Young people are often seeking meaning in their lives; but sometimes older people are still engaged on that search. Perhaps you yourself are such a person. You are looking for what it is that makes life worth living. Perhaps you've looked at several religions and philosophies. You haven't yet found what you want, but you're still looking.

If you are such a person, then could I commend to you the pearl of great price which is set before you today? This pearl is the good news that God loved the world so much that he actually became a part of it, in the person of his Son Jesus Christ; that Jesus spoke the words of God to all who would listen, and still speaks them today through the Gospel to all who will listen; that Jesus, though without sin or fault of any kind, suffered death on a cross; that God's loving purposes for mankind were not defeated by his death, but rather, God raised him up to new and eternal life, and, far from punishing those who had so cruelly abused him, he offers them a place in his kingdom, and shares with them his glory. You will never find another pearl to match this one; and I urge you to make it your own.

Eighteenth Sunday of the Year
FEEDING THE FIVE THOUSAND

Readings Isa 55:1-3; Rom 8:35.37-39; Mt 14:13-21

A large crowd of people had gathered to hear Jesus preach. The disciples were concerned about their welfare: 'Send the people away, and they can go to the villages to buy themselves some food.' But Jesus tells them, 'Give them something to eat *yourselves.*' It may be that he is saying something of the same sort to us today. Many people in Africa are starving; we have all seen the distressing pictures on the television; and we ourselves have the opportunity to give them something to eat, by contributing to the appeal. Very often, it seems, Jesus asks us to do something like this, and very often we respond generously. We acknowledge that it is our Christian duty to feed the hungry. We know also that in feeding the least of his brothers or sisters, we are feeding Jesus himself. Every follower of Jesus surely knows this.

But there are other kinds of hunger. Hunger for the word of God, hunger for meaning and purpose and direction in our lives. No doubt the people in the wilderness were experiencing that kind of hunger. They didn't come to Jesus for a free lunch; that was a bonus. They came to hear what he had to tell them about the Kingdom of God. People nowadays are still hungry for meaning and purpose in their lives.

We can all see much that is wrong with our society: people sadly lacking, it may be in honesty, or chastity, or patience, or tolerance; people too lacking in hope and trust, people in the grip of despair or depression, people consumed by selfishness and greed. How often when we watch the news or read the papers do we say, 'Someone should do something about it.'

Well, perhaps Jesus is telling *us* to do something about it. *You*, he is saying, *You yourselves*, give them something to eat. Not just earthly food; man shall not live on bread alone, but by every word that proceeds from the mouth of God. Give them the word of God for their food, give them the Gospel. Give it to them yourselves, don't leave the matter to your priest, or your bishop, or to a missionary society. To those in doubt, give faith, to those in despair, give hope, to those in grief give consolation, to those who are perplexed give meaning and direction, to those who are alienated give the assurance of belonging.

We may be rather daunted to hear such a command from Jesus. No doubt the disciples were daunted when they were told to feed the five thousand themselves. They didn't feel equipped to do so. They had very small resources, just five loaves and two fishes; and what was that among so many? But Jesus doesn't leave them to do the job unaided. The loaves and the fishes are multiplied by grace, and prove to be more than adequate to requirements. We ourselves may feel ill-equipped. We may not have a degree in Theology, or six years' training as a priest. Who are we to go and tell people the Good News?

If we use what gifts we have, Jesus will multiply them by his grace. Every one of us here has some idea what the Gospel is about. We may not have grasped it in all its fulness; there may be things we are not certain about. But we all have *something*. We all know that Jesus is the Son of God, we all know that he died on the cross and rose again, we all know that he has the power to heal people. We have, as it were, five loaves and two fishes. If we can bring ourselves to share those loaves and fishes with others, Jesus will multiply them in the sharing. We may find ourselves telling people things we didn't even know we knew. That is the marvellous way in which grace works, that is the wonder of the Gospel.

Nineteenth Sunday of the Year
WALKING ON WATER

Readings 1 Kgs 19:9.11-13; Rom 9:1-5; Mt 14:22-33

Have you ever walked on water? I have, many times. Actually it's not difficult. Of course, the water has to be frozen; and this is where Jesus shows his mastery over the elements. He walks on the stormy waters of the Sea of Galilee, as calmly as if they were frozen to ice. No wonder the disciples exclaimed, 'Truly, you are the Son of God.' Perhaps they called to mind the words in the Book of Job, 'Have you entered into the springs of the sea, or walked in the recesses of the deep?' Or perhaps they thought of a verse from the Book of Ecclesiasticus: 'Alone I have made the circuit of the vault of heaven and have walked in the depths of the abyss.' Or perhaps it was simply their common sense that told them that only God could do such things.

Many commentators have tried to give a rational explanation for this incident. Someone has suggested that Jesus was actually walking along the shore, or in shallow water, and in the twilight the disciples thought he was walking on the water. I find it hard to believe that the disciples were quite as stupid as that. Others have suggested that what is described was actually an appearance of Jesus after his resurrection, in his resurrection body. Possibly; though if that was the case you might have expected the evangelists to tell the story in its proper place, as further evidence for the resurrection. Others suggest that the story is merely a symbolic expression of a spiritual truth, that Jesus can save us even amid the stormy waters of trouble.

The fact is, if you don't believe that Jesus is God, nothing in the world will persuade you that he could walk on water, and you will accept any theory, however far-fetched, which explains away the incident. But if you do believe that Jesus is God, there is no difficulty whatever in believing that he could walk on water; except perhaps to wonder why the almighty God should bother to perform what for him would be no more than a party trick. The other miracles of Jesus have a real purpose, beneficial to those involved: a blind man receives his sight, a woman is cured of an issue of blood, a child is raised from the dead. But what useful purpose is served by this miracle?

It has two purposes, as it seems to me. First, it strengthens the faith of the apostles, and incidentally of ourselves. We see it achieve its purpose with the disciples when they bow down and say, 'Truly, you are the Son of God.' It was necessary for Jesus to show the disciples beyond any doubt who he is. The disciples were slow to believe, and several such demonstations were necessary. At the Transfiguration, the disciples saw Jesus for a few minutes as he really is. We are familiar too with the miracle of Jesus turning water into wine. The wedding-guests did benefit from that miracle, but the benefit was secondary. The principal purpose of the miracle was to manifest the glory of Jesus, to show his power over creation. And of course the greatest demonstration of the divinity of Jesus is the resurrection itself. All these miracles then serve to establish our faith that Jesus is the Son of God.

And secondly, the miracle does show us that Jesus can save us, even amid the stormy troubles of our life. I dare say most of us have experienced those storms in one form or another. A loved one falls sick or is taken from us; we cry out, 'Lord, save us, lest we perish.' We lose our job, we fall into disgrace; we cry out, 'Lord, save us, lest we perish.' We are overcome with remorse as we contemplate some bad thing we did, or some good thing we did not have the courage or generosity to do. We cry out, 'Lord, save us, lest we perish.' We fall prey to depression or despair; we are oppressed by loneliness and desolation. We cry out, 'Lord, save us, lest we perish.' And Jesus does indeed walk with us on those stormy waters, waters which he alone can calm; for truly, he is the Son of God.

Twentieth Sunday of the Year
PERSISTENCE

Readings Isa 22:19-23; Rom 11:33-36; Mt 16:13-20

The Gospel teaches us the virtue of perseverance. A Canaanite woman begs Jesus to cure her daughter. He answers her not a word. The disciples ask him to do something for her, if only to shut her up. Still he refuses. She kneels at his feet and begs him, 'Lord, help me.' He replies in a way that may strike us as harsh and rude: 'It is not fair to take the children's food and throw it to the house-dogs.' And still she persists: 'Even the house-dogs can eat the scraps that fall from their master's table.' Jesus, at last, is moved, and grants her request.

The story is of a piece with several others where Jesus teaches his disciples to go on praying and never give up. For example, the story of the unjust judge. He cares neither for God nor man, but a widow keeps banging on his door, asking him to judge her case. In the end he gets so fed up with her persistence that he grants her wish. Or again, Jesus tells of a man who goes knocking on his neighbour's door. He says, 'I've had some unexpected visitors and I have nothing in the house to give them. Let me have some food for them.' The man has already gone to bed and he doesn't want to be bothered, but he has to respond to his neighbour's persistence. He gets up and gives him what he wants.

So Jesus is, in a way, acting out a parable with this woman, showing us how to pray. The essential thing is not to take no for an answer. Don't worry about being polite. Prayer is not a matter of polite requests. Keep banging on the door. Never give up.

This may seem to contradict what Jesus tells us about not pray-ing at great length, in many words. But in fact the woman's prayer is not long or wordy. 'Sir, Son of David, take pity on me.' And when Jesus takes no notice of that she comes up with a shorter one: 'Lord, help me.' You can't get much more direct and to the point than that. It's the prayer of someone who expects an answer, who demands an answer.

Too often in our prayers we are simply thinking aloud, setting our own thoughts in order. 'Wouldn't it be nice if our children came back to Church … poor old auntie is in a bad way with her arthritis … I do hope my brother gets back home safely, the roads are so dangerous these days.' We can go on for an hour like that without actually addressing God at all. If God is listening – and of course he is – he might well say, 'That's all very interesting, but what's it got to do with me?' He might even feel like tiptoeing away and leaving us to it.

One of the longest prayers in the Gospel is that of the Pharisee in the Temple: 'Lord, I thank you that I am not like other men … ' and so on. He goes on at some length. The evangelist remarks that he was talking to himself. The prayer of the publican was very short: 'Lord, have mercy on me, a sinner.' And that was the prayer which was heard. Not just because it was short, but because it was addressed to God. It was a real prayer.

One of the most successful campaigns of our time has been that for Real Ale. Perhaps we should also have a Campaign for Real Prayer. There are lots of real prayers in the Gospels, some of them in this very passage: 'Son of David, take pity on me' or 'Lord, help me.' Or again, 'If you will, you can make me clean,' or 'Save, Lord: we perish,' or 'I believe; help my unbelief,' or 'Jesus, Son of David, have mercy on me!' or 'Lord, that I may see!' All those prayers were real prayers, uttered by real people in real need. And they were all granted.

Twenty-first Sunday of the Year
WHO DO YOU SAY I AM?

Readings Isa 22:19-23; Rom 11:33-36; Mt 16:13-20

Jesus puts a question to his disciples: Who do people say I am? Different people had come up with more or less far-fetched ideas as to who Jesus was: John the Baptist, Elijah, one of the other prophets. The disciples had heard the talk; they knew what people were saying; they also knew it was nonsense. But then Jesus asks another question: Who do *you* say that I am? Peter speaks up: You are the Christ.

He had good reasons for his answer. The Christ, the anointed one of God, had been promised for centuries. The disciples had witnessed those promises coming true in the life and actions of Jesus. Only last week we heard of Jesus healing a deaf and dumb man, fulfilling the prophecy, The ears of the deaf shall be unsealed, and the tongues of the dumb sing for joy. Peter had seen these things, and had drawn the right conclusions. He had his answer ready: You are the Christ.

Now today, Jesus puts the same question to us: Who do *you* say that I am? We could give the same answer as Peter: You are the

Christ, the promised Messiah, the Holy One of God. That would be a perfectly correct answer, and indeed Jesus commended Peter on that answer. Peter was blessed, because it was not flesh and blood that had revealed this to him, but God himself.

We have no quarrel with Peter's answer. But there are many other possible answers. There are dozens, perhaps hundreds, of answers given in the Bible to the question, Who is Jesus? Saint Paul says that he is the power of God, and the wisdom of God. In another place, Paul says, he is the image of God. The Letter to the Hebrews says, he is the radiant light of God's glory and the perfect copy of his nature. Saint John calls him a light that shines in the darkness. Jesus calls himself the Good Shepherd, and the Light of the World, and the Bread of Life, and the Resurrection, and the Way, the Truth, and the Life, and several other titles. An exercise every Christian should do from time to time is to read all these titles, and ponder what they mean. That may seem a bit daunting, but actually we do just that, because whenever some statement about Jesus comes up in the readings we hear it expounded in the homily, and are given the chance to ponder its meaning.

But I wonder if we could not today ponder a question to which the answer is not to be found in the Bible, or in any other book. It is the same question that Jesus is still asking us: Who do *you* say that I am? He's not looking for a ready-made answer. He's not asking, Who does Peter say that I am? or who does Paul say that I am? or even, Who did I myself say that I am? He really wants to know, Who do *you* say that I am? Who am I to *you*? What part do I play in *your* life?

Anybody can answer this question. You don't have to be a biblical scholar, or a theologian; certainly not a priest. A child can answer it as well as an adult.

All you have to be able to do is to look into your own heart, and ask, What difference does Jesus make to my life? He calls himself the Good Shepherd. Is he *my* Good Shepherd? Am I really aware of being fed by him and led along the right path? He is called a light in the darkness. Is he a light in *my* darkness? Does he show me the way in my own darkness and perplexity? Paul calls him the power of God, and the wisdom of God. Does he empower *me* in my weakness? Is he *my* wisdom? Or what *is* he to me?

Twenty-second Sunday of the Year
BAD NEWS

Readings Jer 20:7-9; Rom 12:1-2; Mt 16:21-27

'How lovely on the mountains are the feet of him, who brings good news.' The first line of one of our much-loved hymns, taken of course from the Book of Isaiah. Perhaps somebody should write another hymn, beginning 'How ugly on the mountains are the feet of him, who brings bad news.'

Everybody loves the bringer of good news, and everybody hates the bringer of bad news. It was the unfortunate destiny of Jeremiah to be chosen to be the bearer of bad news. God told him to proclaim the worst possible news to the people of Jerusalem. The Babylonians were going to destroy their city, and carry them off into captivity to Babylon. There was no chance of resisting them; the only hope was to surrender on the best possible terms.

Suppose that during the second world war somebody had gone around saying, 'This is all part of God's plan. He is determined to punish us for our sins, by the hand of Adolf Hitler. It is useless to resist; in fact it is adding to our sins, for we are resisting the will of God. Our only hope is to surrender.' What would people have thought of such a man, or such a message? He would have been the most hated man in Britain.

And Jeremiah was the most hated man in Jerusalem. The army commanders complained to the king that Jeremiah was destroying the morale of the people, as indeed he was. They had him put into prison, and thrown into a pit, up to his neck in mud and slime.

How do you think Jeremiah felt about his mission? What did he say to God in his times of prayer? Was he grateful to God for choosing him to be his messenger? Indeed he was not. He felt as you or I would have felt. He said, 'Why did you pick me for this errand? Couldn't you have picked somebody else? Couldn't you have got me to proclaim news of happiness?' Or to quote his exact words, 'Each time I speak the word, I have to howl and proclaim, 'violence and ruin!' The word of the Lord has meant for me insult, derision, all day long.' Jeremiah didn't enjoy being a prophet. He would gladly have given it up. Indeed, he tried to give it up. 'I used to say, 'I will not think about him, I will not speak in his name any more.'' But he goes on, 'Then there seemed to be a fire burning in my heart, imprisoned in my bones. The effort to restrain it wearied me, I could not bear it.'

If anyone suffers from depression, anyone is grieving, anyone has a heart torn apart by bitterness, resentment, disappoint-ment, despair or self-pity, then I would strongly recommend that person to read the prophet Jeremiah. Jeremiah felt all those things and expressed them more clearly than any other writer in the Bible: 'A curse on the day when I was born! Why ever did I come out of the womb to live in toil and sorrow and to end my days in shame?'

Christ also had to experience all those terrible things: rejec-tion, desolation, pain, even death. He had to experience them on behalf of all of us who suffer pain and are desolate. One day he will be able to tell us, 'Yes, I know what you've been through. I know what it is to say, from the bottom of my heart, 'My God, my God, why have you forsaken me?''

Peter didn't want Jesus to experience those things. He took him aside and began to argue with him: 'God forbid! This must not happen to you.' But Jesus rebuked Peter, because it was neces-sary that Jesus should suffer. Otherwise he would have nothing to say to those who suffer so dreadfully, except, 'Yes, it must be terrible, but I really can't imagine it. I've never experienced anything like that.' God would have remained a God who loved his people, but not enough to become one of them and to share their sufferings, their desolation, their death.

There could be no resurrection without first the crucifixion. And so it is in our lives: we shall never share the glory of Christ unless we are willing to share the pain, nor share in the fruits of the resurrection unless we are willing first to taste the bitter fruit of his passion. That is the good news for those who now suffer and grieve. As Christ says, 'Anyone who loses his life for my sake will find it.'

Twenty-third Sunday of the Year
SENTRY

Readings Ezek 33:7-9; Rom 13:8-10; Mt 18:15-20

Most of you know me as a mild-mannered, gentle old priest but I have to tell you I have a cruel streak in my nature. Sometimes in my cruelty I think what fun it would be to have someone with a speech impediment trying to read today's passage from the prophet Ezekiel: 'Warn a wicked man to wenounce his ways and wepent! Say to him, You wicked wetch, wenounce your wicked ways!'

There would be an irony in having the very person charged with speaking out clearly, being unable to speak distinctly. Some people think the Church is like that. I've often heard people say, The Church should speak out more clearly about this or that. It may be the evils of war or capitalism or abortion or any number of other issues. But it's never the evils which the people complaining are actually committing. Everybody wants the Church to take a stand against the things which other people are doing. If I were to make an inventory of the sins which were actually being committed in this parish, and preach against them, there would be an almighty outcry.

Nobody likes having his or her own faults denounced. I don't like it myself. But we should be a shallow sort of Church if we were forever campaigning about what other people were doing, and didn't look into our own hearts and set about changing what we found there. Our Lord himself tells us that's what we should be doing: not trying to take the splinter out of somebody else's eye, but taking the plank out of our own.

Our Lord also, in today's Gospel, tells us how to avoid one of the faults we most commonly commit. If our brother does something wrong, we should, in the first instance, go and have it out with him alone, between our two selves. So often, when we think we have a grievance against our brother – or, it may be, our sister – we have it out with everyone *except* the person concerned. We tell the butcher, the baker, the candlestick-maker, everybody except the person with whom we are at odds. In this way we deepen the rift that has opened up between us and our neighbour, and involve far more people than is necessary.

Saint Paul backs up our Lord's teaching when he tells us, 'All the commandments are summed up in this single command: You must love your neighbour as yourself.' To refuse to be reconciled to our neighbour, and to involve others in our quarrel, is not to love our neigbbour as ourself. It is not to love our neighbour at all. But to love our neighbour as ourself is, as Paul says, the answer to every one of the commandments.

I would be very happy if this homily actually helped us to love our neighbour. Sometimes people are kind enough to tell me that they liked my homily. Sometimes they are honest enough to tell me that they didn't like it. But the point is, not whether you liked it or not, but whether it changed you. Whether you did anything about it. Whether you came to Mass the next week a different person because of it. The most important part of a homily is what you did about it after it was preached.

So could I ask you, as your response to this homily, to go away and love your neighbour as yourself. Forget the rest of my homily. Don't worry about whether you liked it or whether you didn't like it, whether it was too long or too short, whether it was too funny or too serious. Just love your neighbour as yourself. At the Judgement you won't be asked to give a critique of your priest's homily. You'll be asked, 'Did you love your neighbour as yourself?'

Twenty-fourth Sunday of the Year
SEVENTY TIMES SEVEN

Readings Ecclus 27:30–28:7; Rom 14:7-9; Mt 18:21-35

Have you ever listened to yourself saying the Lord's Prayer? Sometimes I've listened to myself saying it and been shocked to realise that I've been making nonsense of it, by putting the emphasis on the wrong words. 'Forgive us our trespasses, as we forgive those who trespass *against* us.' That's nonsense, isn't it, if we say it like that? It should be, 'Forgive us *our* trespasses, as we forgive those who trespass against *us*.' Do you notice the difference? It doesn't make sense to put the stress on the word against. The only way to trespass is, against. You can't trespass for somebody. The point of the sentence is that we ask for *our* sins to be forgiven, and we acknowledge that the condition of receiving forgiveness is that we are ready to forgive those who sin against *us*.

The fact that we so often garble that prayer is evidence that we haven't really thought through what it means. Perhaps we don't want to do so, because the prayer makes a very uncomfortable demand upon us. We must forgive others from the bottom of our hearts, for all the nasty, mean, low, underhand things they've done to us. We must let them go, put them out of our mind, forget about them. And we don't want to do that.

One little phrase I overhear all too often is : 'I'll never forgive her.' Or maybe, 'I'll never forgive him' – it could be either man or woman. And for what? What dreadful crime has this person done, which rules out any hope of forgiveness? Murdered someone's family? Burned down someone's house? No, all too often it's nothing worse than an unkind word, a thoughtless action, a lack of due courtesy. Regrettable, no doubt, but hardly a hanging matter. Hardly a reason to carry a grudge to the grave.

Our gospel story holds up to us how much we have been forgiven, and how reluctant we are to forgive. The servant owed ten thousand talents. A talent was a gold ingot, worth perhaps ten thousand pounds in today's money; if you're good at sums, you'll be able to calculate how much ten thousand talents would be worth. That servant owed a vast, unimaginable amount.

Have you ever tried to calculate how much we owe God? How much did it cost God to create you and me? In order to make us, he had to make our parents, and their parents, and pretty much the whole human race. And the human race wouldn't have been any use if it hadn't had this planet to live on; so God created the earth. And to make the earth, God had first to make the sun; and to make the sun, God had to make the galaxy, and the whole universe, just so that you and I could exist.

But, you say, he didn't do it just for our benefit; he did it so that the whole human race could exist. But that's neither here nor there. God's love is not diminished by being shared out. He shows us that in the Mass. We can break the sacred bread into as many pieces as we like, but each tiny fragment contains Christ, whole and entire. And on each one of us, personally, God pours out all his love, whole and entire.

If he spent so much love on creating us, how much did he spend on redeeming us? The ransom that was paid for us was not something perishable, like silver or gold; it was the precious blood of God's own Son. It was poured out for us on the cross. It is poured out for us on the altar at every Mass. All he asks in return is that we forgive others as he has forgiven us.

Twenty-fifth Sunday of the Year
LABOURERS IN THE VINEYARD

Readings Isa 55:6-9; Phil 1:20-24.27; Mt 20:1-16

My father-in-law was a farmer in America. It was a dairy farm, so there wasn't a harvest of wheat or barley, but there was a harvest of hay. On that day my father-in-law would hire all the help he could get to bring in the harvest. I remember helping him one year. I believe I worked harder and longer than anyone else, but unlike the other workers, I didn't receive any wages. I didn't expect any. My father-in-law had already given me his daughter; I didn't look for money as well. I was family. His profit was my profit.

It's easy to draw the wrong conclusion from the story of the vineyard in the Gospel. The landowner chose to pay the latecomers as much as those who had toiled all day. Those of us who have been Christians all our lives perhaps see ourselves in the role of those who toiled all day in the sun, and we can, like the men in the parable, grumble at those who come in at the last minute. If their reward will be the same as ours, would we not do better to stay out of the vineyard altogether, enjoy ourselves, and make a death-bed repentance at the eleventh hour?

If we think like that, we show ourselves to be hired hands and not God's family at all. We are not working for wages. We are God's children. Every minute we can spend in the company of our heavenly Father is a great blessing to us. Any work we can do to build up his kingdom is a great benefit to us. The kingdom of heaven is, after all, for our benefit, not for God's. His kingdom is our kingdom. God is not enriched in the slightest by the great harvest of souls which is being gathered into his barns; but how great are the riches he bestows on those whose privilege it is to be his co-workers!

St Ignatius of Loyola well expresses the spirit in which we should labour in the vineyard in his beautiful prayer: 'Teach us, good Lord, to serve thee as thou deservest; to give and not to count the cost; to fight and not to heed the wounds; to toil and not to look for rest; to labour and not to seek for any reward; save that of knowing we do thy will. Who livest and reignest, world without end. Amen.'

Twenty-sixth Sunday of the Year
EMPTYING OURSELVES

Readings Ezek 18:25-28; Phil 2:1-11; Mt 21:28-32

I used from time to time to visit a small religious house, in which one room was set aside as a chapel. In the chapel there was a crucifix; quite a striking metal crucifix by a modern sculptor. It would not be to everyone's taste, but speaking for myself, I found it very moving. Our Lord's body was shown as a hollow shell. You could have put your hand inside, if you'd a mind to. The crucifix spoke to me of Christ emptying himself out for our sake; pouring out his blood, pouring out his life, pouring out everything until nothing was left but an empty shell. It was saying in sculpture what Saint Paul says in words: 'His state was divine, yet he did not cling to his equality with God, but emptied himself to assume the condition of a slave.'

Christ emptied himself; an idea all the more moving when you couple with it another phrase from Saint Paul, that in him all the fullness of God was pleased to dwell. Imagine Christ being full to the brim with God, full to the brim with all the life and all the love in the universe, and then emptying himself out completely for you and me.

Saint Paul doesn't tell us this just for interest's sake. He tells us that in our minds we must be the same as Christ Jesus; that is, we must empty out ourselves just as Christ emptied himself out for us. And surely there are many things in us which need to be emptied out. Christ was full of God; what are we full of? All too often we are full of anger, full of rage, full of spite, full of envy, full of pride, full of greed. If Christ emptied himself, how much more do we need to empty ourselves!

But how do we do it? Suppose, for example, we find ourselves full of anger. How do we empty it out? Let's be sure, first of all, that it's the kind of anger we want to empty out. Sometimes we are perfectly right to be angry. If for example, we saw a grave injustice, or someone abusing a child, we should be quite right to be angry. It would be wrong not to be angry. That kind of anger is no sin; our Lord himself was often angry in the face of injustice.

But all too often our anger is not of that quality. It has nothing to do with a burning zeal for justice. It has everything to do with our own self-importance, our own selfishness, our own irritability. So how do we empty out such anger? When instructing children I sometimes show them an ordinary drinking-glass. I ask them to empty all the air out of that glass. Some of them try sucking it out, but that doesn't work. I assure them it can be done very easily, but they can never figure out how to do it. In the end, I show them. I take a jug of water, and fill the glass. As you fill it with water, so you empty out the air. Easy, when you know how.

So it is with our vices. If we concentrate on the vice, we shall never empty it out. What we need to do is to pour in the corresponding virtue. Suppose we find ourselves full of pride. The only way to drive it out is to fill ourselves with humility. The finest way to acquire humility, and so to drive out pride, is to contemplate a crucifix. I defy anyone to consider how Christ poured himself out for us, and still remain puffed-up with self-importance. In the case of anger, we need to pour in love, and patience, and temperance. When Christ poured out his life for us on the cross, was he angry with those who had betrayed him? No, he loved them with all the love in the universe; and if we ask him to pour his love into us it will drive out every evil thought, and every harmful passion.

Twenty-seventh Sunday of the Year
THE LEASE

Readings Isa 5:1-7; Phil 4:6-9; Mt 21:33-43

Why did the tenants behave so abominably towards the landowner? Because they forgot that he was the landowner. They thought that they themselves owned the land, or ought to have owned it; and they resented having to give over the fruits of the land to someone else. They would have preferred that there was no landownder.

Do we stop to think that everything we have is leased to us? Our property, our families, our bodies, our life itself, are leased to us by God. One day we will have to give them all back, and to give an account of how we have used them. Does that prospect please us, or not? Would we rather that we really did own our own property, and were responsible to nobody for the way we spent our lives?

Would we prefer that there was no landowner? That is to say, would we prefer that there was no God? Surely not; we want a God that we can pray to, someone who can help us in our difficulties and heal us in our sickness, someone who will be a loving father and comfort us in our sorrows. But do we want a God who will call us to account? In recent years the Church has, quite rightly, talked less about a God who punishes, or a God who judges, and more about a God who loves us. I don't want to revive the old harsh ideas about God, but I think we should continue to bear in mind that the God who loves is also a God who expects. A God who expects a return on all the love he has lavished on us. As Isaiah says, I expected my vineyard to yield grapes. Why did it yield sour grapes instead?

What return exactly does God expect? God expects fruit. Have you ever noticed how much fruit there is in the Bible? It begins with someone picking forbidden fruit, and it ends with the offer of fruit from the tree of life to all the redeemed. In between there are all kinds of fruit: grapes, olives, figs, apples, pomegranates. And the word 'fruit' is often used as a figure of speech for other things. For example, Paul tells us that the fruits of the Spirit are love, joy, peace, patience, kindness, goodness, trustfulness, gentleness and self-control. Rather an odd figure of speech, isn't it, to describe such things as fruits? What actually does the word fruit mean?

It means something enjoyed. The word comes from the Latin verb *fruor*, meaning 'I enjoy.' It's hard work planting a vineyard. Isaiah tells us that his friend ' ... dug the soil, cleared it of stones, and planted choice vines in it. In the middle he built a tower, he dug a press there too.' Hard work, and hot work; but he expected the vineyard to bear fruit, that is, something he could enjoy as a result of all his labours.

That is the point of the figure of speech. Love, joy, peace, patience and the rest are things we enjoy. It is obviously more enjoyable to be at peace than to be at war. Kindness, goodness, trustfulness, gentleness are enjoyable things. Even self-control is enjoyable: it is more enjoyable to be in control of oneself than to be out of control. And it's certainly more enjoyable for those who have to live with us.

God enjoys these things as well. He enjoys it when we live at peace with one another. He enjoys it when we exhibit love, patience, kindness, goodness and gentleness. These are a few of his favourite things. These are the fruits he looks to us to bear.

Twenty-eighth Sunday of the Year
THE WEDDING BANQUET

Readings Isa 25:6-10; Phil 4:12-14.19-20; Mt 22:1-14

'So these servants went out on to the roads and collected together everyone they could find, bad and good alike.' Those people out on the roadways have done nothing whatever to deserve being invited to the banquet. They have not pleased the king, or done anything at all to deserve his favour. They are invited simply because the king is determined to have guests at his banquet.

These people represent the recipients of God's grace. Grace is simply a free gift. God offers us his love, his strength, his help, his salvation, an invitation to his banquet, for no reason except that he is a generous God who loves us. We have no right to a place in heaven; nothing we can do could possibly earn it. For that matter, we have no right to expect God's help on earth. If he does walk with us and share our load, if he does hear our cry for help in our pain and distress, then that is down to his kindness rather than to our deserving.

What about the fellow not wearing a wedding garment? We have to understand that it was not a case of his being unable to afford a wedding garment. He could perfectly well have provided himself with the appropriate clothes, but he did not bother. He did not respond to the king's generosity. He represents those who do not respond to God's grace.

Our religion is about God's grace, and our response to it. God's grace comes first: he makes us in his own image, he sends his Son to be our saviour, to teach us God's ways, to take our sins upon himself. He sends his Holy Spirit upon us, he loves us, forgives us, saves us, helps us, strengthens us, delivers us by his grace. But we need to respond to that grace. God does not, after all, drag us into his banquet whether we want to go or not. We can, if we so wish, respond to his kind invitation in an ignorant and churlish fashion. We can, in fact, neglect to put on our wedding garments.

What are these wedding garments? Perhaps they are the clothes of which Saint Paul writes: 'You are God's chosen race, his saints; he loves you, and you should be clothed in sincere compassion, in kindness and humility, gentleness and patience. Bear with one another; forgive each other as soon as a quarrel begins. The Lord has forgiven you; now you must do the same. Over all these clothes, to keep them together and complete them, put on love.'

See how each of those garments represents a response to God's grace. We should be clothed in sincere compassion, kindness, humility, gentleness and patience. God has already shown us each of those qualities in abundance. The whole of human existence is the story of God's kindness to us. He has given us everything we own, even life itself. Should we not show kindness to others? He has shown us his humility through his son, who, though sharing God's nature, humbled himself to become a man, and, as St Paul says, humbled himself still further, to accepting death, death on a cross. Should we not then be humble with one another? 'Compassion' means sharing people's sufferings; and Christ has demonstrated his compassion abundantly by sharing our sufferings on the cross. Should we not suffer with and for others?

Paul talks of gentleness and patience. Has God not been gentle with us? Has he not been patient with us on a thousand occasions? So should we be gentle with one another, and patient with those who provoke us. 'The Lord has forgiven you,' says St Paul, 'now you must do the same.' We know how much we have been forgiven; how can we deny forgiveness to others? Paul begins by saying that God loves us, and ends by telling us, 'Over all these clothes, to keep them together and complete them, put on love.' So love is the overcoat, wrapping itself around all these other qualities and including them in itself: God's love for us, and our response of love for God.

What a splendid outfit St Paul describes! No bride ever wore a more beautiful wedding dress. We could spend thousands of pounds at the best outfitters in town, and not come up with such a suit of clothes. If we put on garments like that, we need have no fear of being cast out of the wedding-banquet.

Twenty-ninth Sunday of the Year
CYRUS

Readings Isa 45:1.4-6; 1 Thess 1:1-5; Mt 22:15-21

In the year 538 B.C. Cyrus, King of Persia, invaded the empire of Babylon and conquered it, annexing it to his own empire. If it helps you to keep the geography straight, Persia is modern Iran and Babylon is modern Iraq. So it was as if the Iranians had invaded Iraq and put an end to Saddam Hussein, as no doubt they would have liked to do. The Babylonians had ruled their empire with great harshness and cruelty. Half a century earlier they had themselves conquered Jerusalem, destroyed the Jews' beautiful temple and carried them away into exile far from their homes. This half century had been a most miserable time in the history of the Jewish people. It was then that the psalmist composed one of the most memorable and moving of the psalms: 'By the rivers of Babylon, there we sat down and wept, when we remembered Zion. On the willows there we hung up our harps. For there our captors required of us songs, and our tormentors, mirth, saying, Sing us one of the songs of Zion! How shall we sing the Lord's song in a foreign land?'

Cyrus put an end to all this. He had a much more benevolent attitude towards his subject peoples. He allowed the Jews to return to Jerusalem. He encouraged them to rebuild the Temple. Then the psalmist sang a very different song: 'When the Lord restored the fortunes of Zion, we were like those who dream. Then our mouth was filled with laughter, and our tongue with shouts of joy.'

As you can imagine, the Jewish people thought that Cyrus was a very great man. He was their hero. The prophet addresses him: 'Thus says the Lord to his anointed, to Cyrus, whom he has taken by his right hand to subdue nations before him: It is for the sake of my servant Israel that I have called you by your name, conferring a title on you though you do not know me.'

'Though you do not know me.' Cyrus had never heard of God; at least, not the God of the Jews. He was not a Jew, he knew nothing of the God of Abraham and Isaac and Jacob. Yet God was using him to further the progress of the kingdom of God. I don't suppose Cyrus ever heard or read the words of the prophet; if he did, he might have said, 'I know nothing of your God; I'm not doing all this for the sake of his kingdom; I'm doing it for my own benefit, to enlarge my own empire.' Nevertheless, he did a powerful amount of good, and the Jews blessed him for it.

Each of us can do a powerful amount of good, to further the progress of God's kingdom. We have the advantage over Cyrus, in that we have heard of God, and we do want to serve him. Still, like Cyrus, we have no idea of the ultimate consequences of our actions, or how they will serve God's purposes. But if we do love our neighbour as ourself, if we are faithful in keeping the commandments, if we are regular in our prayers, if we love our children and try our best to bring them up in the faith and pass it on to them – even if at times they don't seem to take any notice – if we do support the mission of the Church and are generous in sharing our goods with the disadvantaged: then we are doing a tremendous amount for the Kingdom of God.

One of the documents of the Second Vatican Council says, 'While helping the world and receiving many benefits from it, the Church has a single intention: that God's kingdom may come, and that the salvation of the whole of mankind may be achieved.' Every good deed we do, every prayer we utter, is in accord with that intention. We can't see where our faithfulness is leading. One day God will tell us: how our prayer on one occasion averted a disaster on the other side of the world, how our intention at one mass saved a desperate soul from damnation, how much of God's love we were able to channel into the most hopeless of situations. And we shall say, 'Lord, did we really do all that?' And he will say, 'Yes, of course. Whatever you did, for the least of my brothers and sisters, you did for me, and for the furtherance of my kingdom.'

Thirtieth Sunday of the Year
THE GREATEST COMMANDMENT

Readings Ex 22:20-26; 1 Thess 1:5-10; Mt 22:34-40

I don't think St Matthew liked the Pharisees very much. In his Gospel Jesus is always quarrelling with them. In our reading today, the Pharisees get together and, to disconcert Jesus, put to him the question, 'Which is the greatest commandment of the Law?' It isn't clear why such a question should disconcert Jesus; in fact, he has no difficulty whatsoever in dealing with it.

In St Mark, the story is told very differently. To begin with, the questioner isn't a Pharisee. He's a scribe, a member of a rather different set of people. There's no suggestion that he asks his question to disconcert Jesus; on the contrary, he is said to ask it because he had observed how well Jesus answered questions. Jesus gives him much the same answer as in Matthew: 'This is the first: Listen, Israel, the Lord our God is the one Lord, and you must love the Lord your God with all your heart, with all your soul, with all your mind and with all your strength. The second is this: You must love your neighbour as yourself. There is no commandment greater than these.' The scribe congratulates Jesus on his answer: 'Well spoken, Master; what you have said is true.' And Jesus, seeing how wisely he had spoken, says, 'You are not far from the kingdom of God.' For Mark, this is a perfectly friendly encounter.

Why then does Matthew turn the affair into such a hostile encounter? Because, as I already suggested, he doesn't like the Pharisees very much. It can be a shock to realise that before we can understand Jesus, we have to take into account the feelings and prejudices of those who tell his story, and to make allowances for the spin they put on that story. Matthew and Mark tell two very different stories; and for that matter, Luke tells the story in yet a third way.

It is remarkable though that in all three stories, despite the differences in the way they are told, one thing remains very clear: that for Jesus, the most important thing in the world is that we should love God with all our heart and all our soul and all our mind and all our strength; and the second most important thing is that we should love our neighbour as ourself. These commandments are the core of our religion; or as Jesus says, on these two commandments hang the whole Law, and the Prophets also. All the rest is just commentary, spelling out the implications of those commandments.

All the same, the implications of those commandments are pretty formidable when you spell them out, as the Book of Exodus does. We must not molest the stranger or oppress him; we must not be harsh with the widow or the orphan, or with the poor; in short, with any of those people who are vulnerable or marginalised in our society. And some of those people can be very awkward, and difficult, and ungrateful, and deceitful. We are not on that account excused from loving them.

'You must love your neighbour as yourself.' A hard commandment to keep. It would be a lot easier to keep if it only applied to certain classes of people; but everyone is included. The lawyer who asked Jesus the question in Luke's version of this story, went on to ask, 'But who is my neighbour?' He got an answer which perhaps he would have preferred not to hear. Even the Samaritans, the hated and despised enemies of the Jews, were his neighbours. Who are our Samaritans? Who are the ones we think ought to be excluded from the commandment? The person who did us that bad turn? The one who was so rude to us? It would be pleasant it these people were exempted from the commandment; but they are not. We must love them.

If it is hard to love our neighbour as ourself, how much harder it is to love God with all our heart and soul and mind and strength! It would be easier if we only had to love God with half our heart; to come to Mass when we felt like it, to say our prayers when we were in the mood, to do his will if it accorded with our own inclinations. But it is in the nature of a commandment that it tells us to do something whether we like it or not.

Nevertheless, these are the commandments, not of a tyrant but of a loving God. They teach us the way of light, the way of life; and God himself, knowing our frailty, gives us his grace to follow them as we could not without his aid. Like the most indulgent of fathers, he forgives us when we fail, and raises us up and restores us in his Son Jesus Christ, who came, not to those who find the commandments easy to keep, but to people who find them very difficult, to you and me.

Thirty-first Sunday of the Year
PRIDE

Readings Mal 1:14–2:2.8-10; 1 Thess 2:7-9.13; Mt 23:1-12

Our Lord warns us today against the sin of pride, and commends to us the virtue of humility. We should not seek the place of honour at banquets and the adulation of the crowd. If we aspire to be great, we should be the servant of all; if we wish to be exalted, we should humble ourselves. The Church has always faithfully reflected our Lord's teaching by considering pride to be the worst of the sins, indeed the root cause of all the other sins.

Now, I was taught that there are three kinds of pride: pride of face, pride of place and pride of grace. Pride of face is simply being proud of your face, or more generally, of your body, of your physical appearance. If you find yourself afflicted by this kind of pride, you can do one of two things. First, you can do what I once did. Go on an archaeological dig, excavating skeletons. I remember digging up a skull, and as I scraped the earth away, a huge and juicy worm came out at great speed from its eye-socket. And I thought, I may be a handsome devil now, but in a few years' time I'll be just as repulsive as this fellow. And that's one remedy for pride of face.

If you haven't got the time for archaeology, might I suggest instead that you contemplate the sight of Christ on the cross. A young man in the prime of life, he offered himself up to be flag-ellated to a bloody pulp, to be turned into a human scarecrow. As Isaiah says, 'Without beauty, without majesty we saw him, no looks to attract our eyes; a thing despised and rejected by men, a man of sorrows and familiar with suffering, a man to make people screen their faces.' And with that image in your mind, ask yourself if you have any right to be proud of your appearance.

Pride of place is being proud of who you are, of your position in life. Proud, perhaps, of being rich, or of having an important job, of being a very important person. Rather like those scribes and Pharisees who loved to be greeted obsequiously in the market squares and having people call them Rabbi. The remedy for that kind of pride, should it afflict you, is again to contemplate Christ dying for us on the cross, and perhaps to call to mind the words of Saint Paul: 'Always consider the other person to be better than yourself ... In your minds you must be the same as Christ Jesus. His state was divine, yet he did not cling to his equality with God, but emptied himself to assume the condition of a slave, and became as men are; and being as all men are, he was humbler yet, even to accepting death, death on a cross.'

Pride of grace is being proud of the graces you have been given, that is the gifts you have received from God. It may well be that you are kind and generous and brave and honest and chaste and humble and possessed of every virtue. Those virtues are admirable. But never forget that those virtues are gifts granted to you by God. If you become proud of those gifts, and think you are better than other people because of them, then those graces have become a snare for you. I suppose we are all guilty of be-ing proud of our graces when we criticise others who fall below our standards. We read in the papers about callous burglars, or politicians caught with their hands in the till or sometimes with their hands in more unseemly places, or people guilty of lout-ish behaviour, and perhaps we despise those people. That isn't right. By all means let us despise their actions, but the people themselves are to be loved and prayed for, not despised. Christ did not despise *us*; he loved us and gave up his life for us, praying all the time for sinners. It's an old saying, and a true one, that we should hate the sin but love the sinner.

Can we do that even when the sinner is sinning against ourself? It may be possible to love a sinner, provided that he's sinning against somebody else. It may be possible to *forgive* someone who does sin against ourself; indeed we claim to do so every time we say, 'Forgive us our trespasses, as we forgive those who trespass against us.' But Jesus tells us to do more than forgive them; he tells us to love them. 'I say this to you: love your enemies and pray for those who persecute you.' Do we dare to try?

Thirty-second Sunday of the Year
WISE AND FOOLISH VIRGINS

Readings Wis 6:12-16; 1 Thess 4:13-18; Mt 25:1-13

Let's get one thing out of the way to start with: those ten girls were not bridesmaids. We are the victims of a mistranslation. Saint Matthew calls them ten virgins; this may mean no more than 'girls', but they were not the bridesmaids. No doubt there were bridesmaids at the wedding, but the job of bridesmaids is to wait upon the bride. The bridesmaids would have been inside with the bride. The job of *these* girls is to wait upon the groom. They were to wait for his arrival and conduct him by lamplight into the wedding-hall.

Those girls represent us. We are waiting for the arrival of the bridegroom, that is our Lord Jesus Christ, who as our creed teaches us *will* come again in glory to judge the living and the dead. The expectation of his coming again is expressed not only in the creed, but permeates the whole Mass from beginning to end. One of the invocations in the penitential rite says, 'You *will* come in glory with salvation for your people.' Our Eucharistic acclamations tell us 'Christ has died, Christ is risen, Christ *will* come again'; or else we say, 'We proclaim your death, Lord Jesus,

until you come in glory'; or we pray, 'Lord Jesus, come in glory.'
One of our Eucharistic prayers says that we are 'Ready to greet
him when he comes again' – a phrase surely referring to today's
gospel; another Eucharistic prayer says, 'looking forward to his
coming in glory'. The *Libera Nos*, the prayer we insert into the
Lord's Prayer, asks God to 'Protect us from all anxiety as we wait
in joyful hope for the coming of our Saviour, Jesus Christ.'

Christ will come again, but when? The early Christians thought
he would come very soon, certainly within their own lifetimes.
In particular, Saint Paul, at least in his early days, believed and
taught that he and his flock would not die, because Christ would
come and put an end to death before it was their time to die.
As the years passed, some of the Christians at Thessalonica and
elsewhere did of course die, either through persecution or in
the natural course of things. And this caused some distress and
perplexity. Had they missed their chance of partaking in Christ's
kingdom? Some of the most touching stories about the two
world wars concern those who were killed actually on armistice
day, just before the outbreak of peace. A few more hours, and
they would have enjoyed life and peace and victory. As it was,
they missed it by a whisker. Was that the case with those early
Christians who had died, as people thought, on the eve of the
return of Christ?

Saint Paul assures the Thessalonians that this is not so. God
will raise those dead Christians to life to take their place in the
kingdom with those who are left alive until the Lord's coming.
And when will that be? Paul refers to be drawn into predictions
of dates and times. The important thing is to be awake and sober
and ready when he comes; and that echoes the teaching of many
of our Lord's own parables, notably today's: 'Stay awake, because
you do not know either the day or the hour.' Suppose Christ came
at midnight tonight: would we be ready to meet him?

So often we behave as if we had all the time in the world at
our disposal. We make all kinds of good resolutions about what
we ought to do one day: we ought to patch up that quarrel, we

ought to get in touch with that old friend, we ought to get round to making a confession, we ought to keep that promise, we ought to give up that bad habit. And so we will, tomorrow. Our readings today teach us, Don't leave it until tomorrow. Tomorrow may be too late. Let's do it today.

Thirty-third Sunday of the Year
TALENTS

Reading
Prov 31:10-13.19-20.30-31; 1 Thess 5:1-6; Mt 25:14-30

It's often remarked that you can prove anything from the Bible. You can read on one page that you should honour your father and your mother; and on another, that if you do not hate your father and your mother, you cannot be a follower of Christ. Or again, Jesus tells a young man, 'Go and sell everything you own, and give the money to the poor, and come, follow me.' And he commends his disciples who have given up houses, brothers, sisters, fathers, children and land to follow him. Is that then what Jesus wants of you and me – to give up everything, money, property and family, everything we have, to follow him?

Not necessarily. Because we have to balance this demand with what Jesus tells us in the Parable of the Talents. Three servants are entrusted with various quantities of talents, which are actually gold ingots worth thousands of pounds each. One is given five, one is given two, the last receives only one. These are things which are not to be renounced, but rather cherished and nurtured, for the sake of the one who has given them to his servants.

Each of us has talents which are on no account to be given up. A certain young man had a training as a scholar, and an academic career. On being ordained to the priesthood, he had resolved to renounce that part of his life and devote his whole time to parish ministry. But someone with greater discernment than himself said, 'No – your learning is your talent. You must not on any account give it up. Otherwise what are you going to say to Jesus at the Last Judgement? Here's your talent back. I dug a hole and buried it in the ground?'

Our whole lives are talents loaned to us by God. They do not belong to us; one day they will have to be given back to their true owner. Those who say, 'It's my life, and I shall do as I like' are missing this basic point. The woman in our first reading is a great asset to her husband: from her he will derive 'no little profit', she brings him 'advantage and not hurt.' It can be objected that she has no life of her own, she is seen only in terms of the benefit she brings to her husband. No doubt she illustrates the limitations of the appreciation of womanhood in the Old Testament. But she also stands for ourselves, both men and women, who are called to live our lives not for our own benefit, but in the service of God, to bring him 'advantage not hurt.'

God is interested in what we make of our lives, and in what benefits we bring to his kingdom. Too often when we examine our consciences we think only of the bad things we have done: the angry word, the unworthy thought. These things are regrettable, but also forgiveable. What can be much more serious is the utter failure to do anything positive and worthwhile with our lives. Someone once said (and like all great truths, it is an exaggeration) that there is only one mortal sin: not to ask someone to join the Catholic Church. It is no great effort to ask a friend to come to church with us, or to share our faith with a workmate or family member. And yet many people never make even so small an effort to build up Christ's Church. Such a failure might be compared with that of the idle servant who could not even be bothered to deposit his talent in the bank.

Some of our most precious talents are our families: husbands and wives, parents and children. Gifts to be cherished, but ultimately to be returned to God. Think of it: to be able to say at the Last Judgement, 'Lord, you gave me, it may be five children, or two, or just one. I have brought up those children, had them baptised, educated them in the faith, taught them your commandments, showed them how to love, encouraged them to receive your sacraments and to walk in your ways. Now I give them back to you, in a far better state than when I received them.' Will God not say, 'Well done, good and faithful servant! Enter into the joy of your master!'

Thirty-fourth Sunday of the Year
CHRIST THE KING

Readings
Ezek 34:11-12.15-17; 1 Cor 15:20-26.28; Mt 25:31-46

I once met a shepherd, out in the fields, working his sheep. I say again, I *once* met a shepherd. It was the only occasion in my life when I have encountered such a person. Jesus would have met shepherds every day. When he applied the title to himself, 'I am the good shepherd,' he was using an image which was very familiar to his hearers. Probably many of his hearers were shepherds. Some would be farmers who employed shepherds. All of them would know shepherds. Nowadays shepherds are rather rare. An image which in Jesus's day was commonplace and self-explanatory now needs to be commented on.

The same can be said about kings. If you read the Bible you must be struck by what a lot of kings there were about. Every city seemed to have its own king: there was a king of Salem, a king of Sodom, a king of Tyre, a king of Sidon. It was natural enough to refer to God as a great king. Nowadays very few countries have kings, and those of us who have are beginning to wonder if they're such a good thing. A king has become something unusual, something historical, something rather quaint. The same could be said about the title 'Lord.' The British House of Lords, as formerly constituted, has been abolished; and many would say, not before time. Should we still be referring to God as 'Lord' or

'King'? Do these titles mean anything nowadays? Would we not be better off calling God 'Senator' or 'President'?

We should make a great mistake if we did. A senator, or a president, is someone we elect. If these people don't live up to our expectations, we can get rid of them and elect someone else. A King, or a Lord, is someone we're stuck with, whether we like him or not. And that is the reality of our relationship with God. We do not choose God. He may choose us, but we have no choice. We can choose to obey him or not, but there is no alternative God to whom we can transfer our allegiance. God is there, whether we like it or not, the only source of creation, the only source of goodness and grace. As he says himself through the prophet Isaiah, 'Am I not the Lord? There is no other god besides me, a God of integrity and a saviour; there is none apart from me.'

It is remarkable how St Paul takes the images of God's power, of God's uniqueness, of God's universality, of God's Lordship and Kingship, even of God's ruthlessness, and applies them to Jesus. A president, or any elected authority-figure, must behave constitutionally. He may not murder or banish his political enemies. Such behaviour would be that of an ancient tyrant. But such is the behaviour of Jesus. He will do away with every sovereignty, authority and power – that is, he will destroy every rival to his absolute rule. 'He must be king until he has put all his enemies under his feet, and the last of the enemies to be destroyed is death.'

Paul is using for his imagery the political world of the Roman Empire in which he lived, a world where resistance to authority let to sudden and certain death. It may shock us to hear Jesus, the gentle shepherd, the meek lamb, being described in such terms. Perhaps we have allowed our ideas of Jesus to grow rather bland. Or perhaps we really do feel that we should no longer picture him as an authoritarian King who insists on obedience to his demands. Such an image of Jesus, we may feel, is outmoded.

And yet what are his demands? That we should feed the hungry. A third of the people on earth today are starving. The hungry are not outmoded. That we should welcome the stranger. The world is full of refugees, driven out from their own countries to seek asylum in ours. Strangers are not outmoded. That we should care for the sick. Whole countries are afflicted with AIDS, and diseases like TB are making a comeback. The sick are not outmoded. That we should go to see those in prison. The prisons of the world are full. Some prisoners are rightly held in custody for the evil they have done, others are prisoners of conscience, some are simply victims of miscarriages of justice. All are in need of Christ's compassion. Prisoners are not outmoded.

Christ's demands amount to this, that we should visit, care for and love all the suffering people of the world. And in this he is very different from a tyrant, for no tyrant ever issued such demands. His demands are the demands of Love, and they lead to eternal life.